Music
worldwide

Elizabeth Sha...

CAMBRIDGE
UNIVERSITY PRESS

CAMBRIDGE
UNIVERSITY PRESS

University Printing House, Cambridge CB2 8BS, United Kingdom

Cambridge University Press is part of the University of Cambridge.

It furthers the University's mission by disseminating knowledge in the pursuit of education, learning and research at the highest international levels of excellence.

Information on this title: education.cambridge.org

First published 1998
17th printing 2015

Printed in the United Kingdom by Printondemand-worldwide, Peterborough

A catalogue record for this publication is available from the British Library

ISBN 978-0-521-37622-8 Paperback
ISBN 978-0-521-37481-1 CD

Additional resources for this publication at www.cambridge.org/delange

Illustrations by Fran Sewell

Cover illustration by Helen Manning

Contents

Introduction

Do you know anybody who can honestly claim that they do not like music at all? I doubt it. The infinite variety of music which has existed all over the world since the evolution of man must mean that everyone can find some music which pleases them.

Our expectation of what makes good music is based on previous experience. We accept *some* new sounds – features of harmony, instruments or rhythms – but feel ill at ease if *nothing* is familiar. On the other hand, a musical diet which is completely predictable becomes boring, even to the most conservative listener. If we only listened to things we knew, we would all still be listening to nursery rhymes!

What we require from music is a blend of the expected with the unexpected, although the proportions may vary according to the taste and personality of the individual.

Many people in the West, when first experiencing Indian classical music or Arab music, for example, find it very difficult to understand. Similarly, people brought up in *those* cultures find it difficult to appreciate Western classical music.

However, there are some basic similarities between all types of music. All music is based on melody and rhythm in some way. It is the organization of these elements which produces the varieties of mood and expression. All music appeals to the spirit and the emotions, as well as to the intellect. It can inspire, entertain, soothe or excite, and has been used in most of the cultures of the world to enhance religious events and other special occasions, as well as to make everyday life more enjoyable.

In order to create music which will not be forgotten as soon as the last note has been performed, rules and patterns needed to evolve on which musicians could base their creative ideas. These rules and patterns – together with the enormous variety of musical instruments found all over the world – determine the basic differences between the music of various cultures. In this book we shall explore some of the sounds, styles and instruments of the world's many musics.

Africa

We are concerned in this chapter with what is sometimes termed **Sub-Saharan Africa** – roughly speaking, Africa south of the Sahara Desert. North Africa shares with it many points of interaction. On the other hand it belongs historically and culturally to the Arab world.

Rhythm

Rhythm is the most important feature of African music, and this has had a great effect on popular music all over the world. As a result of the slave trade which began in the 16th century, African rhythm styles spread all over the Caribbean and the southern states of America. Africans were taken against their will and forced to work on cotton and sugar plantations, and they took their music – particularly their exciting rhythms – with them.

In European music, the first beat of each bar is regarded as the strongest. In $\frac{4}{4}$ time, for example, the 1st beat is stressed most, then the 3rd. In a lot of African music, it is the 2nd and 4th beats, the 'off' beats, which are clapped or stressed. The same custom has persisted in jazz, rock, reggae, soul, gospel and other popular music styles – all African-influenced.

Assignment 1

Listen to recordings in some of the popular styles listed above – as wide a variety as possible, using any recordings to which you or your school have access. As you listen, practise clapping the 'off' beats.

Much African music appears to be in $\frac{12}{8}$ time. There are four main beats to each bar, but each beat divides into three. This is also an important feature of jazz and blues.

Assignment 2
CD TRACK 1

Listen to part of a dance from Ghana, called *Atsiagbeko*. It tells of acts of bravery in war, and has complicated percussion rhythms set over a fast $\frac{12}{8}$ marked by the *kidi* (small drum):

An important performer in this type of music is the 'master drummer', who improvises patterns which tell the dancers which steps to perform. As the track proceeds, you will hear an emphasis on the second and fourth beats, the 'off' beats. Try clapping on these beats, as you did in assignment 1.

Ewe drum ensemble from Ghana with (left to right) axatse (rattles), gankogui (double bell) and four barrel drums: atsimewu (master drum), sogo, kidi, and kaganu

In African music it is common for several rhythm patterns to be played at the same time, sometimes with each part apparently in a different time signature. The way the parts sound against each other gives a very exciting effect, known as **polyrhythm**. The next assignment is a simple example.

Assignment 3 Divide into groups of three, each choosing an instrument with a contrasting sound. Look at the three lines of music; each person takes one line. First play lines 1 and 2 together, and then lines 1 and 3. Then play all together.

Notice that to performer 2, performer 1 appears to be playing in four-time, but performer 3 thinks performer 1 is playing in three-time.

Assignment 4 Now divide into groups of five. One person improvises a 'master drummer' part to go with line 2 (above), and another improvises a part to go with line 3. Put all the lines together in various combinations, sometimes all playing together, sometimes taking it in turns to stop. Also, change lines with each other. Compose an exciting piece of rhythm music in this way.

Assignment 5 Here is an African dance rhythm, an extract from a dance called *Adzogbo*, from the republic of Benin.

bell

kaganu (small high-pitched drum)

kidi (small drum played with a stick)

♩ = bounce the stick off the skin

♩ = mute the sound by leaving the stick on the skin

Divide into groups and select instruments as similar as possible to those described. Play each part separately first, and notice that, played on its own, the bell part appears to be in four-time, the *kaganu* in three-time, and the kidi in $\frac{6}{8}$ time.

Assignment 6

Sometimes a group of drummers will start a rhythm pattern, followed half a beat later by another group playing the same pattern.

Play this rhythm pattern in two groups, using instruments with contrasting sounds. It would be a good idea to try the pattern all together at first.

Make up a pattern of your own and play it like this with a partner.

6

Talking drums – rhythm and language

Drums are not only used to add rhythmic vitality to songs, dances and ceremonial music. In many parts of Africa they have been used for centuries to convey messages.

Most African languages are 'tonal', which means that the *pitch* of the spoken word is as important as the word itself. The same syllable, pronounced at different pitches, can mean different things.

Drums need not only play rhythms, they can play at varied pitches too. This is sometimes achieved by tightening and relaxing the strings which hold the skin onto the body of the drum – as with the hourglass drum shown in the picture. Sometimes changes in pitch can be made by pressing the skin with the other hand, or by using different-sized drums.

A skilled drummer can reproduce so accurately the pitches of speech in his own language, that it can *sound* like speech to his listeners. Messages are often sent in this way. At celebrations, the ancestors of the family can be remembered and praised through the talking drum rhythms, and on official tribal occasions, chiefs are often praised.

hourglass drum

Many chiefs have their own special drummers, and the skill is passed from father to son. Repeated rhythm patterns transmit messages more and more strongly, and this has also been brought into the African popular music called *highlife*, found in cities. Talking drums form part of the instrumental line-up of many highlife groups. Sometimes talking drums give instruction on how dance steps must be performed.

Assignment 7
CD TRACK 2

Listen to this short example of talking drums, recorded at Tamale in northern Ghana.

Now assemble some drums of different pitches, and see if you can reproduce some short, well-known phrases, or the names of class members, using a combination of rhythm and pitch.

Next, experiment with a larger drum, pressing on the skin with one hand while playing with the other, to produce rhythms at various pitches.

When trying to imitate talking drums, you will have to think very carefully about the rise and fall of your voice, and copy it as closely as possible. Would someone from another part of the country, whose accent and intonation differ from yours, be able to understand your attempts at talking drum messages? Try to guess what other members of the class are 'saying' with their drums.

Music, language, the rhythm of life

All African art forms – music, dance, drama and visual arts – are closely linked with the language of the tribe or area. The arts form a vital part of everyday life, and give social and tribal groups a sense of pride in their own identity. Even the instruments used, which are made from materials easily found in the locality, vary from tribe to tribe. Africans feel that instruments

7

are not just played – they 'speak a language'. And so African musicians prefer to play instruments made in their own district, and tuned to their own scale.

Music-making is a group activity in which everyone joins. Each tribe has its own songs and dances and its own instruments. Every special event in the life of an individual or group is celebrated by the appropriate songs. This preserves traditions, and gives support to those going through an important development in their lives, because they know that the same songs have been sung in the same situations for many generations. There are songs to celebrate birth – and songs for a person who has just died, to help him or her move happily into the spirit world.

Assignment 8

Make a list of the events in a person's life which you think would be marked by a special song in Africa. Then make a list of songs or music which are traditionally used in Britain (or your own country) to mark special events.

Vocal music at work

Songs are used to accompany repetitive physical work, especially when done by groups of people working together. The rhythm of the song is made to match the rhythm of the work, and the songs help to pass the time more pleasantly when boring jobs have to be done.

These work-songs were carried by slaves to the southern states of America, and the style of the songs remained even when the language used eventually became English. These songs were called 'field hollers' and were an important means of communication, because the slaves were allowed to sing while working, but not talk.

A fairly common form of African song, which has still remained in use in work-songs and spirituals in America and the Caribbean, is the 'call-and-response' song. It is also found in African church music. A leader sings phrases which are answered by a chorus – sometimes singing an exact repeat and sometimes an answering phrase. Quite often, the chorus part is a repeated refrain, sometimes sung in harmony.

Songs are also used as a means of teaching children. There are counting songs, songs which explain how things must be done, and even 'punishment' songs. These must be sung over and over again by the child, as he or she puts right something which has been damaged by carelessness.

When puberty is reached, there are songs which explain the facts of life, and set out the differing roles of men and women in family life.

Assignment 9

Make up a teaching song for young children. You could use the call-and-response technique. Alternatively, make up a punishment song.

Story-telling songs are a means of preserving tribal history, as each generation of children learns the legends and tales of the deeds of their ancestors. In some cultures, there are special castes or families of musicians whose job it is to teach, through songs, the history and legends surrounding the tribe.

Sometimes, when Africans are worried or troubled, it has been known for them to continue to sing for several days, in order to 'sing away' their troubles. This has an obvious link with the blues songs of America.

Assignment 10   The melodies of African songs are based on scales in which the intervals are comfortable to sing.

Play or sing this lullaby, called 'Ushuru'. It is from Buganda, and is based on a five-note scale. A translation of the words is given below.

1. You are on my back when I grind and when I spin,
   Come down my baby, my back is sore.

2. I, the baby's mother, will come back to see him,
   Mother will bring bread and milk in her arms.

Assignment 11   In white-dominated South Africa, music has always been an emotional outlet, and a means of showing unity. Here is a street song from Soweto, which makes reference to the events of June 1976, when students protested against a government attempt to standardize the language spoken in Soweto schools. There were many arrests, and tear gas was used, and the fighting lasted for three weeks. Sing or play this song:

2. We're not afraid of the prison walls,
   It is for freedom that we go now. *(repeat)*
   A heavy load, a heavy load,
   And it will take some real strength. *(repeat)*

3. They took our land, they took our homes.
   How much longer will they bleed us?
   A heavy load...

4. In Soweto they shot us down,
   But we will rise up united.
   A heavy load...

African scales

In traditional African music, there is no fixed scale as European musicians know it, no theory involving fixed combinations of tones and semitones. In 'equal temperament', the intervals between all semitones of the chromatic scale are exactly equal. This is important to European music because it depends so much on chord-based harmony, which would sound 'out of tune' if the semitones were not all equal. The 'untempered' scale is found more often in musical cultures in which vocal melody is all-important. The human voice often slightly varies the pitch of certain notes, without the singer realizing it, to suit the contour of the melody line.

Since African musicians pitch the melodies of their songs within a range in which it is comfortable for them to sing, and tune their instruments accordingly, there is no fixed pitch either. Song melodies and instrumental music are based on whatever scale suits the needs of the performers.

Many tribes base their melodies on a five-note scale. Five-note, or *pentatonic* scales are used in folk-music all over the world. Music based on a five-note scale is often easier to sing, as there are usually no semitones. A typical five-note scale found in West Africa might correspond to European pitch something like this:

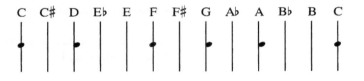

Assignment 12

Discuss ways in which you can make up your own untempered five-note scale. You could use bottles filled to different levels with water, or some other way of making different pitches. First you will need to fix the lowest and highest notes an octave apart, then space out the four notes in between. You could use an inexpensive bamboo flute, or even a recorder, and make up your own scale by modifying the fingering, so that you produce notes which do not exactly correspond in pitch to the Western scale.

Improvise some melodies using your scale, and compare your results with those of other class members. When you have improvised your melody on your 'instrument', sing it. Do you find that your vocal version begins to slip back into the scale that you are accustomed to hearing? You may have to ask your classmates to tell you, as you may not notice it yourself.

Harmony

European harmony is based on fixed pitch, and requires equal temperament. The African musician thinks of the harmony line as part of the melody, and as such it is equally important. Even when the harmony appears to sound chordal, in fact each line is regarded as a melody.

Tribes can be grouped according to their preferences in harmony. Some sing the same melody four notes lower, some sing it five notes lower, and these groups never use the interval of a third. Some groups sing the melody in parallel thirds, but never use accidentals in the lower part, even if they should occur in the upper part. This means that the intervals created are sometimes major thirds, and sometimes minor thirds.

Assignment 13
CD TRACK 3

Listen to some cult music of the Blekete Cult from Ghana. Are the vocal harmonies mainly thirds, or mainly in fourths and fifths?

Although there is no bass part in this extract, there is an implied feeling of harmony. See if you can 'sing in' a bass part. How many different notes do you need to sing?

All these harmonic ideas are found in West Africa, from Senegal to Cameroon. This is the main area from which the slaves were taken, so these concepts of harmony have influenced blues and jazz.

The 12-bar blues is a chord sequence based on the chords of the tonic, subdominant and dominant. The melodies which are accompanied by a 12-bar blues sequence usually feature a mixture of major third and minor third intervals. Much Western popular music is based on this chord sequence, particularly the rock music of the 1950s and 1960s.

Assignment 14

Play through the 12-bar blues below, using any suitable combination of instruments. See if you can make up another melody to go with the chords. Also make up some alternative bass-lines.

Assignment 15

Make a list of pop music which is based on the 12-bar blues chord pattern.

African music today

In city areas all over the world, there is a tendency to reject traditional art forms in favour of Western pop and rock, which can be heard on radio, TV and films. But traditional musicians still visit the cities, and in West Africa a musical style has evolved which combines both. This is called *highlife*, in which a calypso-like tune is backed by a combination of Western and traditional African instruments. Highlife bands often involve members of different tribal groups, and the highlife styles vary slightly from country to country. Sometimes talking drum messages are incorporated into highlife music.

Highlife harmonies are based on the chords of the tonic, subdominant and dominant, which tend to be repeated in a regular pattern. The vocal line is often sung in parallel thirds.

Assignment 16
CD TRACK 4
CD TRACK 5

Listen to two short extracts of African popular music and then answer the questions below.

The first track is called 'Mosese 2000', and is performed by the group Somo Somo. This is in the 'soukous' style, from Zaire, and is influenced by the rumba (a dance style which first became popular in the 1930s).

The second track is 'Duke', by Kantata, a group led by Ghanaian guitarist George Darko. They call this style 'asiko', and it is a fusion of highlife with international popular music styles. The song is about a young man living and working abroad, not wanting to return empty-handed to his home village, where he was regarded as a model of success.

(a)   Discuss which of these extracts you find most exciting and why.
(b)   Which extract is based on the chords of the tonic, subdominant and dominant?
(c)   Which sounds Caribbean or Latin-American in style?
(d)   Which has a strong off-beat stress?

Assignment 17

Learn to play these typical highlife rhythm patterns:

Assignment 18

Highlife band

Play one of these rhythms over and over again on a drum or other percussion instrument. Record it on cassette or program it onto a keyboard.

Using piano, guitar or keyboard, add chords, based on a repeating sequence of tonic, subdominant and dominant. Record the rhythm pattern plus chords. Now compose a melody in highlife style, to go with your chords.

(This is just a suggestion of a method of composing in stages. You may prefer to achieve the same result by working in a different way.)

Instrumental music

An enormous variety of instruments is used in Africa – usually made by the musicians to suit their particular tradition, style and taste. The materials used depend on what is readily available in each area. Musicians treat their instruments with great respect, and are said to 'teach them to speak', rather than learn to play them. Instruments are tuned to suit the player's language; musicians do not like to use an instrument – however similar it may appear to be – if it has been made in a different area, as its 'language' will not be the same.

Assignment 19

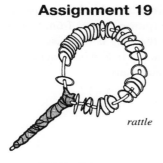

rattle

Look around for things with which to make your own instrument. Here are some ideas which might help:

On the left you can see a rattle, made in Kenya from a wire coat-hanger, threaded with bottle tops. You could use ring-pulls from drink cans. The handle of the Kenyan instrument is wound round with an old inner tube.

Wooden blocks cut to different lengths and threaded on string could make a xylophone, or rubber bands stretched across an oblong tin could make a simple harp. If you make a pitched instrument, tune it to a pentatonic scale of your own choice.

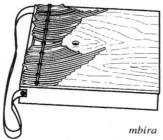

mbira

African thumb pianos can be found all over the continent. They are called by many different names. The Ibo of Nigeria call it an *ubo*. It is tuned to a pentatonic scale, and the body is made out of a gourd. Elsewhere, instruments based on a similar principle, but with rectangular boxes sometimes replacing the gourd, are called *sansa*, *likembe* or, in Tanzania, *mbira*.

As the name 'thumb piano' suggests, these instruments consist of metal or bamboo strips which are flicked with the thumbs of both hands. Try to work out how these instruments are tuned so that the strips produce the required notes. (When you 'twang' a ruler, how can you produce different notes?)

Assignment 20
CD TRACK 6

Listen to the sound of this mbira, made by Tanzanian Hukwe Zawose out of old car seat springs. This instrument has 66 plucked metal tongues, and the notes also produce a buzzing sound. The track is called 'Safari na Muziki' (Walking with music).

Assignment 21
CD TRACK 7

Next, listen to this xylophone music played on an instrument similar to the one pictured below. The wooden notes rest on gourd resonators. Towards the end of the extract, which other percussion instrument can you hear? This piece is played by a Lobi musician from northern Ghana.

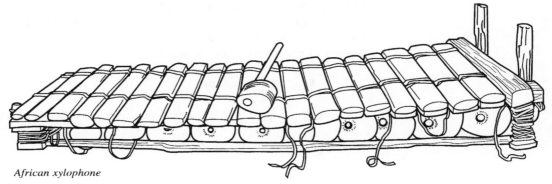

African xylophone

The *kora* is a very beautiful African instrument with a resonating chamber made from a large gourd, cut in half and covered with skin. A hole is cut to let the sound out. The 21 strings are plucked by the musician's thumbs and forefingers. Koras are usually only played by men, and the playing skills are passed from father to son. The kora pictured below is from Gambia.

Assignment 22
CD TRACK 8

Listen to this extract from a song called 'Laminba', accompanied by kora, and describe the sound of the kora. The performer is Foday Musa Suso, a *griot* (praise-singer) from Gambia, and the song is in praise of a wealthy man who is generous to musicians.

kora

African perspectives

Africa is a vast continent, made up of many different countries and hundreds of different cultures. It would be impossible to cover all its musical traditions individually in this book; all we can do is look at certain aspects of African music.

We must remember that much of North Africa, sometimes termed 'Oriental North Africa', has been dominated by the Arab and Islamic cultures, and so will require separate study. Another country with different cultural traditions is Ethiopia, as it has been mostly Jewish or Christian since the time of Christ.

Ethiopia

Christianity was the Ethiopian state religion from AD 333, and monasteries were the centres of learning. Music was part of that learning, and a system of notation was devised involving dots, dashes and other signs, in addition to letter notation from the Ge-ez alphabet. The signs were not meant to show exact pitch, but to act as a memory aid to those who already basically knew the melody. The signs were also intended to give instructions on the manner of performance. For example:

- ●   Detached note

- ∪   Sing in a low deep voice, or hum at the lowest register

- ∫   Upward glissando

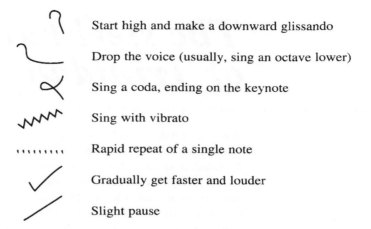

	Start high and make a downward glissando
	Drop the voice (usually, sing an octave lower)
	Sing a coda, ending on the keynote
	Sing with vibrato
	Rapid repeat of a single note
	Gradually get faster and louder
	Slight pause

Assignment 23

Look at the above list. For as many of these instructions as possible, write down the equivalent signs used by Western musicians – i.e. in staff notation. Not all of them have an equivalent, and for some you may need to choose a pitch (any pitch) in order to demonstrate the notation.

Assignment 24

In some modern styles of Western music, signs like those used in Ethiopia are used to show how to perform a piece of music. Scores that use this approach are called **graphic scores**.

Make up, or choose, a short melody. Draw a line to describe the rise and fall of the melody. Use some of the Ethiopian signs – or make up some of your own – to describe glissandi, repeated notes, etc. Sing or play the melody. Exchange your graphic scores with other class members, and see if you can perform each other's.

Do you find it easier or harder to perform from a graphic score than from conventional notation? Can melodies be passed on as accurately? Under what circumstances would it be easier, or more effective, to use a graphic score to organize a performance?

Ras Tafari

Ethiopia is regarded as the spiritual home of the Rastafarian religion. The Rastafarian movement started in Jamaica in the 1930s, at the time of the crowning of the Prince Regent Ras Tafari (meaning Head Prince) as Emperor Haile Selassie of Ethiopia.

The Jamaican nationalist leader Marcus Joseph Garvey taught Jamaicans to be proud of their black African heritage. Garvey believed in one black God, and when he left for America in 1916, he prophesied, 'Look to Africa for the crowning of a black king. He shall be the redeemer!'

Therefore, when Haile Selassie was crowned, Jamaican Rastafarians believed him to be divine. They searched throughout the Bible for other signs, believing that the Bible had been wrongly translated by white people.

The rest of the world was not much aware of the Rastafarian religion until the late 1960s, when the music of Jamaican Rastafarian Bob Marley, and his group The Wailers, became popular. The words of Marley's reggae music expressed Rastafarian ideas, and his fine musicianship made his influence spread all over the world.

Look out for recordings by Bob Marley, Peter Tosh (one of the original Wailers) or other Jamaican Rastafarian singers.

The steel band music of Trinidad

When we think of steel band music, we tend to think of the Caribbean islands, but actually steel band music originated from only one island, Trinidad. It has now become popular all over the world.

It is likely that the first steel drums – or pans, as they are called – were made from oil drums left by the Americans during the Second World War. Old oil drums were left in many places all over the world, but only in Trinidad were they turned into musical instruments.

Music forms an important part of the lives of Trinidadians and, like many other people all over the world, they made instruments from anything they could find. During the last century, bamboo poles, of which there are plenty in Trinidad, were used to make 'tamboo bamboo' bands. The hollowed poles were cut to different lengths, to make notes of different pitches. The smaller ones were beaten with sticks, the larger ones bounced off the ground, to an accompaniment of saucepans, bottles, and anything else that would make an exciting rhythmic sound.

At first, the making of steel pans was rather experimental. But gradually, ideas were pooled, and groups of pan makers formed bands. Pan makers experimented to find the best way of arranging the notes on the oil drums, which were cut to different lengths to make high or low sounding drums. They continue to make modifications and improvements to this day. Each band has its own followers and fans, much like pop musicians or football teams in other parts of the world.

The Carnival in Port of Spain (capital of Trinidad) is the most important steel band event of the year. In addition to steel bands, groups of people in spectacular costumes dance and parade in the streets. There are competitions for the best bands and the best costumes. Musicians and costume designers spend a whole year practising and planning for the next Carnival.

London's Notting Hill Carnival was inspired by the Caribbean carnivals, particularly the one in Port of Spain.

Assignment 25

The steel pan must be one of the best examples of recycling that can be found in the world of music!

Look around for ways of recycling discarded articles to make percussion instruments. You may be lucky enough to find a car brake drum or hub-cap lying around, and this is something very often used to add to the percussion accompaniment in steel bands. However, please make sure it really is discarded!

Assignment 26

Choose a cassette, record or CD of steelband music, calypso music or pop music. Form small groups, each person with a percussion instrument (preferably 'recycled') with a contrasting sound. Make up a percussion accompaniment which sounds effective with your chosen music. Each group could perform to the class, perhaps competing in the same way that steel bands compete at Carnival.

Steel band on a Caribbean beach

The Pantastics – award-winning steel band of Littleover Community School, Derby, on their trip to the Ukraine (Musical Director: Anne Johns)

At the first carnivals, some steel pans were hung around players' necks, but mostly they were mounted on great platforms on wheels, which were pushed along by their supporters. Nowadays lorries are usually used.

How the pans are made

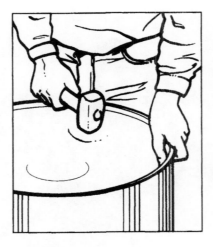

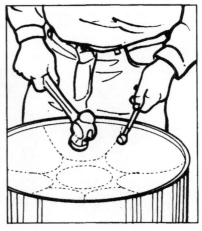

1 Sinking
The oil drum is turned upside down, and the base is beaten with a short-handled sledge-hammer to stretch the metal into a concave curve.

2 Grooving
The positions of the notes are marked out with chalk, and then grooved out with a steel punch, hit with a hammer.

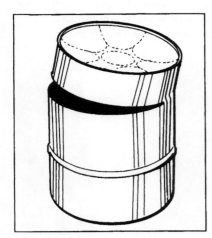

3 Cutting
The pan is cut to the correct length – the shorter the drum, the higher the sound.

4 Burning
The steel is tempered by burning, and then cooled with water to produce a better sound.

5 Tuning and fitting
The pans are tuned so that each note is exactly the required pitch. They have to hang freely, so holes are usually drilled in the sides so that wire can be tied in a loop and hung from hooks on a stand. Basses, which are whole oil drums, are usually supported on sections of motor tyre, or on hard rubber pads.

Making sticks

rubber band

2

soprano stick

3

The sticks used to play steel pans are made from lengths of dowel or bamboo, and rubber bands (or, in the case of bass sticks, sponge rubber balls). The sticks wear out constantly and need frequent repair, so players have to learn how to make their own.

Soprano sticks should be about 16cm long, and can range in thickness from 6mm to 10mm, according to preference. A thick rubber band should be wound around the tip of the stick so that there are about three layers of rubber. The rubber then tapers down the stick with the end tucked in. The lower-sounding pans have longer sticks with thicker tips.

Assignment 27

Practise winding some steel band sticks, for the various types of pans. Even if you do not have a set of steel pans at your school, your sticks could be used for playing some types of xylophone or glockenspiel. Listen to the sound of your sticks, and decide which are the most successful. It takes a bit of practice to make good sticks.

The Pantastics steel band from Littleover Community School, Derby, on their Rhineland Tour

Steel pans produce a unique sound. They are made in a full range of size and pitch, all having a similar timbre – in the same way that the string section of an orchestra contains instruments of varying sizes but similar timbre. The sound of a steel band can consist of complex and exciting rhythms, formed by a combination of short rhythmic phrases and chords. But soft, smooth melodic phrases can also be produced, with a full range of musical expression.

On the next two pages you can see descriptions of different types of pans, showing the range and layout of the notes. Most school steel bands will not have as many pans as this, but it does not matter. Beautiful music can be produced with a small set of pans, or by combining pans with other instruments. Even if you have no pans at all, you can still get some idea of the feeling of playing in a steel band by using xylophones or glockenspiels, as many of the playing techniques are similar.

Types of steel pans

The design and naming of pans varies greatly. Many of the names relate to voices and instruments of similar pitch. The ranges of notes shown here are the most usual ones, though they can vary from one maker to another.

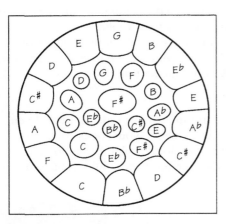

Sopranos

These may also be called 'tenors', sometimes 'ping pongs'. They have the largest range of notes, and usually play the main melody. The highest notes are so small that they are not very reliable for sustained notes which require the player to 'roll' the sticks like a drum roll, but they are perfectly adequate for faster passages.

range:

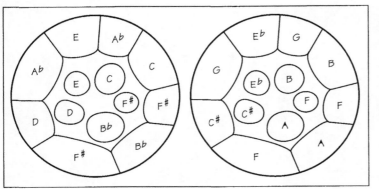

Double altos

These may also be called 'double seconds', or 'double tenors'. One player plays both drums. They are usually used for an alto melody, and sometimes take over the tune when the sopranos are playing a descant part.

range:

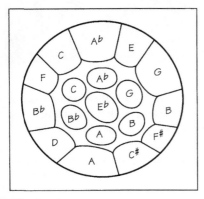

Single altos

These are used to play two-note rhythmic chords rather than melodies.

range:

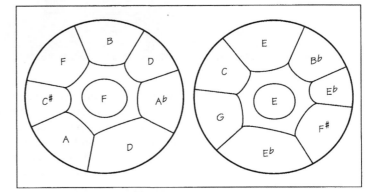

Guitars or double guitars

These are also double pans, each cut from half an oil drum. They can play two-note rhythmic chords, 'strumming' to fit in with the alto part, or they can play a tenor melody.

range:

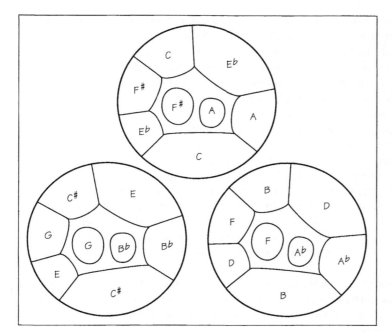

Cellos or triple cellos

These are a set of three pans at tenor pitch, and are about half of the length of an oil drum. They are mainly used for tenor melodies as they are more resonant than the guitars or cellos. They can be very effective duetting with the double altos, or doubling an important bass part.

range:

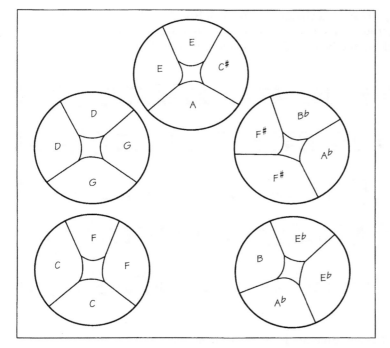

Basses

In order to produce the full range of notes necessary, one player manages five or even six pans. Bass parts can be simple chord-roots, or rhythmic scalic melodies.

range:

Playing steel pans

If you do not have a set of steel pans, you can practise these techniques using xylophones, glockenspiels or chime bars. When playing the pans, the sticks should be held loosely, but not so loosely that you throw them across the room when playing fast passages – something which is quite possible, especially when playing the basses! The pans should never be hit hard, as this not only sounds terrible, but can also ruin the pans if it happens often. Sustained notes should be played by means of 'rolling' – striking the note rapidly with alternate sticks, as in a drum roll.

It is quite a good idea to familiarize yourself with the location of the notes by playing a few scales on each pan. When playing scales and melodies you must sort out which stick you are going to use for each note, in much the same way as a pianist works out the most effective fingering for a passage of music. It is important to get into the habit of using both hands equally. With traditional pieces you will notice that in each, patterns and shapes recur in the positions of the notes on the pans, and you will find it progressively easier to memorize the music the more you play.

Assignment 28

Practise 'rolling' for four counts on each note of a scale: C D E F G A B C. Try starting softly and gradually getting louder, while making sure all the notes sound smooth and even. (This technique can be practised on steel pans or xylophone.)

Assignment 29

Now apply the same technique to 'Banana Boat Song'. The long notes should be 'rolled', the short ones played with a single stroke. Work out which stick should be used for each note according to its position on your pan(s).

Assignment 30
CD TRACK 9

Listen to 'Banana Boat Song' on the CD, and play along with the recording. Join in after the introduction:

Assignment 31
CD TRACK 10

Listen to 'Linstead Market' on the CD. Practise the melody. If the notes on your pan are roughly in the same positions as in the diagrams on pages 20–21, use the left and right sticks as indicated. If not, work out your own left/right arrangement. If possible, play along with the band. Come in after the introduction and play two verses.

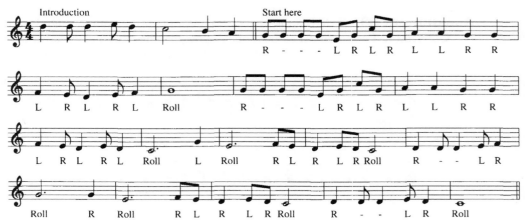

You will have noticed in the last two tunes that phrases of music are often repeated in Caribbean music – sometimes exactly, sometimes with a different ending. Notice also the syncopated rhythm.

Assignment 32

Make up a tune of your own and practise it (it could be in Caribbean style). Work out which notes should be 'rolled', and how to distribute the single-note strokes between the right and left sticks.

Steel bands do not always have to play Caribbean-style music. Any music can be played, so long as it is carefully arranged to preserve the style and mood of the original. Even in the early days of steel band festivals in Trinidad, in the 1940s, bands were playing complex arrangements of orchestral works from the 'classical' repertoire.

Young performers at the Notting Hill Carnival

23

Playing the basses

It is usual at first to play the simple root note of the chord (see opposite). Since the bass player has to manage anything from three to six pans – usually five – it is best to start with something simple and then invent variations, taking care that they fit in well with the style of the piece, and with the other parts.

Assignment 33
CD TRACK 11

Here is the tune of 'Jamaica Farewell' with the chords written underneath. Find a partner; one of you play the tune, and the other the root note of each chord. Try out some rhythmic variations, taking turns to play the bass.

Assignment 34

Now play this melodic bass-line to 'Jamaica Farewell'. Make up some melodic bass-lines of your own to go with the tune.

Playing the chord rhythm pans

The single alto and the cello or guitar pans have several functions in a steel band:

1   They fill in the middle harmonies by playing two-part chords.
2   They provide rhythmic variations.
3   They can create atmosphere and special effects. The combination of chord drums playing softly or loudly increases the dynamic variation of the band as a whole.
4   At times they can play their own melody, or passages of double alto melody or triple cello melody when those parts need to be brought out more strongly.

24

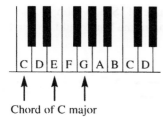

Chord of C major

Most of the time, the alto and cello/guitar parts are based on chords. In its simplest form, a complete chord, or triad, consists of three notes. The lowest note of the triad, from which the chord takes its name, is called the *root*. The middle note is called the *third*, and the upper note is called the *fifth*.

When arranging the notes of the triad for alto and cello pans, it is usual to give the alto the root and the third, and the cello the root and the fifth, or the third and the fifth.

Assignment 35

Play these chords on a keyboard or piano, and then with a partner on alto and cello pans (or xylophones if you have no pans).

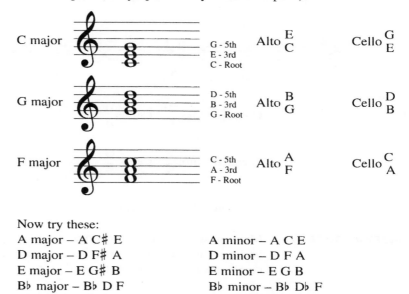

C major	G - 5th / E - 3rd / C - Root Alto E/C Cello G/E
G major	D - 5th / B - 3rd / G - Root Alto B/G Cello D/B
F major	C - 5th / A - 3rd / F - Root Alto A/F Cello C/A

Now try these:

A major – A C♯ E   A minor – A C E
D major – D F♯ A   D minor – D F A
E major – E G♯ B   E minor – E G B
B♭ major – B♭ D F   B♭ minor – B♭ D♭ F
E♭ major – E♭ G B♭   E♭ minor – E♭ G♭ B♭

Remember that when playing pans with note letters written on them, G♭ will usually appear as F♯, and D♭ as C♯, etc.

Rhythm and bass

A good combination of bass and chord rhythm pans is very important to the successful sound of any steel band. In small bands, with no double alto or triple cello pans, the bass and rhythm forms the entire accompaniment to the soprano melody and so will give the band its distinctive style. Here is a simple example of a bass and chord rhythm combination, which would fit most Caribbean folk-style tunes:

Assignment 36

Form groups and try this rhythm pattern to the tune of 'Sloop John B'. Instruments such as xylophones, glockenspiels or chime bars could be used if you have no pans.

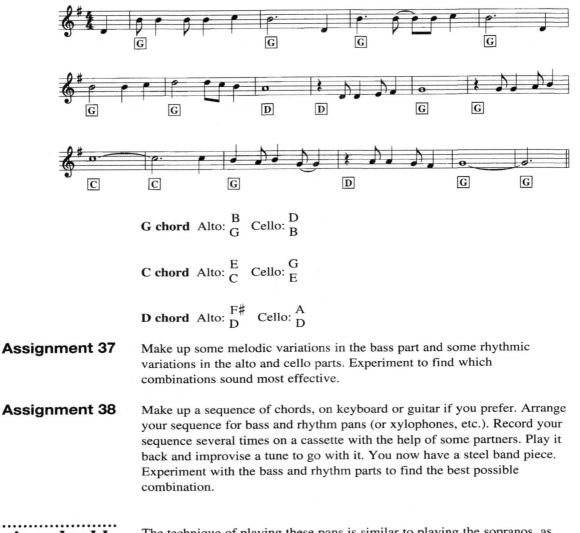

G chord Alto: $\frac{B}{G}$ Cello: $\frac{D}{B}$

C chord Alto: $\frac{E}{C}$ Cello: $\frac{G}{E}$

D chord Alto: $\frac{F\sharp}{D}$ Cello: $\frac{A}{D}$

Assignment 37

Make up some melodic variations in the bass part and some rhythmic variations in the alto and cello parts. Experiment to find which combinations sound most effective.

Assignment 38

Make up a sequence of chords, on keyboard or guitar if you prefer. Arrange your sequence for bass and rhythm pans (or xylophones, etc.). Record your sequence several times on a cassette with the help of some partners. Play it back and improvise a tune to go with it. You now have a steel band piece. Experiment with the bass and rhythm parts to find the best possible combination.

Playing double alto and triple cello

The technique of playing these pans is similar to playing the sopranos, as these are also melodic drums but at alto and tenor pitch. It is more important than ever to work out the distribution between right and left sticks, because the distance to be covered between the notes on the two double alto drums and the three triple cellos is greater, and you cannot afford to get into a muddle or the rest of the band will be carrying on without you! The double altos and triple cellos can sound very effective playing duets with each other.

Assignment 39
CD TRACK 12

Follow the score, and listen to 'Long Time Gal'. Notice how the double alto and triple cello parts fit together with the soprano. Play the piece afterwards, substituting other instruments where necessary.

26

Repeat ℅ to ℅

Repeat ℅ to ℅

Putting it all together

Now that you know something of the function of each type of steel pan, let us try to put together a calypso-style piece in the way that it might be played if the band had to play from the back of a lorry in a parade, or at a dance or barbecue. Under these circumstances the players need to keep playing almost without thinking about it. And the leading soprano player has to improvise, or make as many repeats, as the situation demands. Therefore, a repetitive chord sequence is what is needed, with rhythmic chordal parts arranged to make people want to dance. Let us take the piece called 'Just a Little Bit', and build it up from the bass.

Assignment 40

Start with the bass part, accompanied by a drummer:

When the bass and drummer have played their sequence twice, bring in the chord rhythm drums:

Then bring in the triple cello, and after that the double alto:

Lastly, let the soprano play the melody. The phrases can be repeated at will – and variations can be composed in other parts as well as the soprano.

Assignment 41
CD TRACK **13**

Play 'Coconut Woman' along with the CD, or on your own from the score. You can use this score as a basis, inventing your own rhythmic and melodic variations.

Arab music

By the end of the fourth century and the beginning of the fifth century the Roman Empire was beginning to crumble, and in the east the Arabs were gradually gaining power. They showed themselves to have great intellectual ability, and a strong culture in which music was considered to be important. Arab music has been influenced by the folk-music styles of various parts of the Arab world, which includes North African countries as well as those of the Middle East.

Folk-music

The style of much of the folk-music from North Africa and the Middle East has remained almost unchanged through the centuries to the present day. This is particularly true of the nomadic people such as the Bedouin, who have not been exposed to the music of other races because of their desert lifestyle, and also of the Moroccan Berbers, living in the Atlas Mountains.

Assignment 42
CD TRACK 14

Listen to this dance music from the *Rwayss* poet-musicians of the Moroccan Berbers. The melodic instrument leading the call-and-response is the one-stringed version of the *rabāb*. What other types of instruments can you hear?

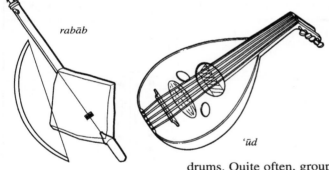

rabāb

'ūd

Arab folk-music is mainly vocal. Like the music of sub-Saharan Africa it has always been used to celebrate events in the lives of individuals and communities. Each ethnic group has its own folk-music, which each generation learns by listening and copying.

Arab community folk-music does not use a wide range of notes, often not extending beyond a 4th or 5th. But it does involve strong rhythmic patterns using hand-clapping and drums. Quite often, group singing is in the call-and-response style, and includes short melodic phrases, often repeated.

Assignment 43
CD TRACK 15

Listen to this folk-song from Tunisia, including voices, oboe and percussion. Notice the small melodic range. Describe what happens in each section of the music.

Assignment 44

Sing this wedding song. Since words are not available, you will have to make up your own, or sing to 'la'. Add drum parts and hand-clapping. Notice that the melodic range is a 5th.

Assignment 45
CD TRACK 16

Listen to *Cerga*. This is a Turkish folk-dance. The instruments include a violin instead of a rabāb, and an 'ūd. Which other instruments can you hear?

Another type of folk-song found in Arab countries is the *epic song*. These are story-poems, performed by a solo singer and accompanied by a rabāb, a fiddle with one or two strings. Epic songs have kept alive stories of heroes and historic events, and have influenced the 'art' or 'classical' music which developed in the courts of local rulers. Poet-composers would compete with each other in the performance of verses made up on the spot.

Assignment 46
CD TRACK 17

Listen to 'Ahbil nra ad dik nmum', performed by Berber musicians. What type of instrument accompanies the soloist, and which instrument joins in with the chorus in this example?

Maqām

In Arab classical music, the modes or *maqāmāt* (plural of *maqām*) are the equivalent of Western scales. However, they have different combinations of tones and semitones, and even include quarter-tones (a quarter-tone is half a semitone). There is no absolute fixed pitch – as is true of both African music and Indian classical music, and also of music from other cultures. The pitch of the tonic may be chosen to suit the performers, who base their melodies on the maqām. There is also a certain amount of pitch variation in some of the intervals of the maqām, or the melodies based on it, as different musicians perform it in their own way. Since the accompanying string instruments are unfretted, or have movable frets, this does not present a problem.

In Arab music, the octave is not divided into equal semitones like those of Western music. The Arab scale consists of two octaves, divided into quarter-tone intervals, and the complete range of possible notes in the two octaves is called a *jadwal*. Each octave is called a *diwan*. However, no maqām uses all the possible quarter-tones. In fact, Arab melodies, as we heard in the folk-music, use a fairly narrow range of notes, usually a *tetrachord* (four consecutive notes), or a *pentachord* (five consecutive notes). The diwan is divided again into half-octaves, called *ajnās*, and the melodies are usually composed using only one *ajān* (singular of ajnās) at a time.

Here are just a few of the ajnās, with the size of the intervals marked below ('1' means '1 tone'). You will notice that each ajān has a name. Usually Arab music is not written in notation, but in order to indicate quarter-tones to people brought up with Western notation, the sign ♭ is used to mark 'half-flats' – notes flattened by a quarter-tone instead of a semitone.

Assignment 47
CD TRACKS 18–20

qānūn

1 Listen to this 'ūd music, *Taksim Hussayni* (track 18). *Hussayni* is the name of the maqām.

2 Listen to the music in maqām *Nihawand* (track 19), played on the qānūn, pictured here.

3 Listen to a short extract from variations in the same maqām (track 20), played on the *nāy*, an end-blown flute.

Comment on the mood, texture and style of each piece.

Assignment 48

Take an unfretted string instrument, such as a violin or cello, and place your fingers on the string so that quarter-tones are produced. You can produce quarter-tones on the guitar by pulling the string sideways slightly as you place your finger on the fret, but it is a little more difficult than using an unfretted instrument.

Assignment 49

Choose an ajān, and compose a melody in the style of the music you have heard. Bear in mind that, in Arab music, phrases are often repeated – exactly or with only slight variation. If you are making up a melody on an instrument with fixed pitch, such as a keyboard, choose an ajān which does not use quarter-tones.

Performance and heterophony

A typical performing group would be a singer with a single instrumentalist or a small group. The melody is all-important, and when several musicians perform a melody together, each may play it slightly differently, for instance in how they choose to ornament it. This is called *heterophony*.

Assignment 50

Form groups of three or four and choose a melody to play.
- Each of you may vary the tempo slightly where you think it would suit the melody, as long as you stay broadly together.
- Each of you should put in grace notes, trills and decorations where you think they would sound right.
You are now playing heterophonically.

Īqā'āt – rhythmic cycles

The art music of the courts was a mixture of ideas from all over the Arab world, but the dominant feature was always the Arabic language and Arab poetry. The rhythm of both folk and art songs is based on Arab poetry, which has a regular pattern. There are fixed rhythm patterns or cycles called *īqā'āt*, which are used to accompany songs and other music. Here are a few of them. Like the melodic modes, they all have names.

Al thaquīl al awwal – 16 beats

♩ ♪ ♩ ♪ ♪ ♩ ♪ ♪ ♪ ♩ ♪ ♩ ♪ ♪ ♪

Al thaquīl al thānī – 16 beats

Ramal – 12 beats

Muḍā'af al-ramal – 24 beats

Assignment 51

Clap these rhythm cycles through. Do you find it difficult to keep together? If so, work out why. What do Western musicians write into a rhythm pattern to help them keep together?

Assignment 52

Make up a short tune, or use one you have already played earlier in this chapter, and try out each of the īqā'āt to see which one fits it best. You may need to change the tune to make it fit the *īqā'* (singular of īqā'āt) exactly.

Music in the world of Islam

The Muslim religion began with the birth of the prophet Mohammed in the small oasis town of Mecca in Western Arabia in AD 571. By 1258 it had spread from the borders of India and China in the east to Spain and the Atlantic coast in the west.

From the musical point of view, the spread of Islam resulted in a great exchange of ideas, as the folk-music of each area influenced the classical music, and the various musical styles were accepted, absorbed and passed on by the Arabs. Musicians and other artists travelled widely, and were highly valued by the aristocracy.

Many instruments used in Arab and Islamic countries are also found in India and many parts of Europe and Africa. For example, the inventor of the most famous Indian instrument, the *sitar*, was in fact a Persian.

There has been a great deal of discussion about whether music should be permitted in the Muslim religion. The holy book, the *Qur'ān*, does not give an answer on the subject. On the one hand, Islamic peoples have developed very complex and refined musical styles, influencing many other cultures. On the other, many Muslims feel that music is associated with a wish for a life of pleasure, and that performances by women, especially when dancing is involved, are indecent.

However, there are three ways in which music is used to enhance the religion, and is generally accepted:

1 The Call to Prayer, known as the *Adhān*, in which the *muezzin* (caller) chants from the minaret-balcony at the top of a mosque. This is performed five times a day to call the faithful to prayer, and is a setting of seven lines of text, made into twelve lines of music.
2 The chanting of the Qur'ān. This has developed from the chanting of pre-Islamic poetry. Its purpose is to enhance the text, and make it more memorable.
3 Special festival music, such as the special melody called the *Fazzaziyat*, which is sung during the month of fasting, Ramadan.

The music of India

Assignment 53
CD TRACK 21

sāraṅgī

Listen to part of a *jugalbandi* (duet) played by Ustād Rais Khan playing the sitar and Ustād Sultan Khan playing the *sāraṅgī*. *Ustād* means 'master' when applied to Muslim musicians. *Pandit* is the equivalent word used if the musician is a Hindu. These two masters of their respective instruments here improvise on a collection of notes which make up the *raga* known as Yaman Kalyan. Notice:

1 The different sounds of the two melody instruments, the sitar and the sāraṅgī. Which instrument do you think is plucked, and which bowed?
2 How the musicians take it in turn to play answering phrases, and then each plays softly when the other takes the lead.
3 The great amount of decoration and embellishment – the notes and phrases are not played in a straightforward way.
4 The *drone* – a continuous note sounded by the drone strings on the sitar and also by an accompanying instrument, the *tamburā*.
5 The gentle, steady rhythm maintained by the *tablā*, a pair of drums.
6 The range of different sounds achieved by the tablā player.

Indian sounds

This piece of music sums up many of the qualities valued in Indian music. Melody is all-important. The improvisations rise and fall against the almost hypnotic hum, or drone, of the continuously sounding tonic note in the background. This provides the harmony, and unique texture, of Indian classical music.

Almost any performance of Indian classical music will contain these three basic elements: melody (one or more instrumentalists or singers), a drone, and rhythm (most often played on tablā).

Hindustani ensemble with (left to right) sitar, sarod, tamburā and tablā (pair of drums)

Assignment 54   You can adapt a guitar to imitate a tamburā by tuning the lowest E string down to D. Then play these notes on the open strings:

low E tuned
down to D

open 3rd
string

open 2nd
string

Find a partner. One of you play the tamburā drone while the other improvises a melody using only these notes, in any order or rhythm: D E F♯ A B D'. These are the notes of the raga Bhupali, which is the same as the pentatonic scale. We will study ragas in more detail later.

Assignment 55
CD TRACK 22

Listen to this extract from a performance by Pandit Shiv Kumar Sharma of raga Bhupali. In this passage the solo instrument is the *santūr*. As you listen, look at the picture of a santūr below. Then make a list of instruments found in other parts of the world which are similar to the santūr, pointing out the similarities and differences.

Playing the santūr

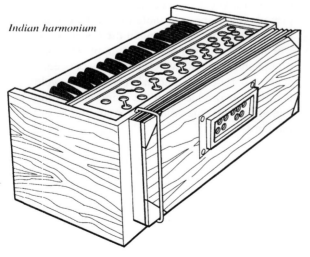

Indian harmonium

The most popular Indian keyboard instrument, the harmonium, was originally taken to many parts of the world, including India, by missionaries, to accompany their hymns. However, all musical cultures continually absorb new ideas, often from other parts of the world, and in India the harmonium quickly became a favourite instrument, particularly for accompanying vocal music. Light-classical vocal pieces, such as *ghazals*, which are settings of Urdu love poems, are very popular with Indian audiences.

Organizing the elements of music

Western music

In Western music, the notes are named after the first seven letters of the alphabet. If you start on C and play up to the next C, using only the naturals (the white notes on the piano), you hear the sound of a major scale. If you start on any other note, you have to substitute some sharps or flats to make it sound correct. 'C' is always at the same pitch, which we call 'concert pitch'.

In Western music, as we have seen in previous chapters, all the semitone intervals are the same size, and the black notes on the piano have two names – for example, F♯ is the same note as G♭. Every note of a Western scale can be made sharp, flat or natural, according to the wishes of the composer.

Most Western music is based on the major scale or the minor scale. Classical music is mostly written down, because harmony is an important part of Western music, and the harmony consists of changing sequences of chords or the interweaving melodies of counterpoint. Western classical music is often performed by large numbers of musicians forming an orchestra, and there is no opportunity for improvisation, as the composer writes all the harmonies and the musicians read the music.

Indian music

In Indian music the names of the notes of the scale are:

sa ri ga ma pa dha ni sa

But *sa* can be pitched anywhere. It does not even have to be exactly in tune with the pitch of any particular note. The pitch of *sa* is chosen by the main singer or instrumentalist to suit his or her voice or instrument, and the accompanying musicians tune their instruments to the pitch of the chosen *sa*.

In Indian music, some notes of the scale are always natural. These are *sa* and *pa*, and they are called *shudh,* which means 'pure'.

Some notes – *ri, ga, dha* and *ni* – are allowed to be flat but never sharp. The word for flat is *komal,* which means 'soft'.

The only note which is allowed to be sharp – but never flat – is *ma*. The word for sharp is *tivra*.

In vocal or stringed instrument music, the komal and tivra notes can be sharpened or flattened to slightly different degrees to suit the needs of each raga. But now that the harmonium is so popular, equal temperament has become more usual.

Indian classical music usually involves a small group – a main performer (for instance a sitar player or a vocalist) accompanied by a tamburā to provide the drone, and tablā to add the excitement of rhythmic improvisations in the faster sections. The main performer and the tablā player improvise on the chosen raga (which is a cross between a scale and a melody) and *tala* (or rhythm cycle). Harmony is produced by the rising and falling melody against the constantly sounding *sa* of the tamburā.

Learning, the Indian way

In ancient times, the princes and maharajas of India encouraged musicians to pursue their art, as music was an important part of court life and good musicians were highly valued. Fathers would pass on their own style of singing and playing to their sons and disciples, and to a large extent this custom still persists. Musicians are said to belong to a particular *gharāna*, which really means a group of musicians studying at a particular place and being influenced by a particular master. Traditionally, although women could study music, they did not become professional performers. Some instruments, such as the tablā, were not considered suitable for women to play.

Music teacher and tablā student

The traditional method of learning was, and still is, mainly by listening, imitating and memorizing. However, there is a method of writing pitch, as an aid to memory, called *sargam* – using the names of the scale notes to write a melody. The names of the scale notes are: *sa, ri, ga, ma, pa, dha, ni, sa*. This is how three octaves would be written:

Ṣ Ṛ Ġ Ṃ Ṗ Ḍ Ṇ S R G M P D N Ṡ Ṙ Ġ Ṁ Ṗ Ḋ Ṅ Ṡ

Most of the melody would be played or sung in the middle octave.

Singers often use the sargam names for vocal improvisations, and teachers often sing a phrase in sargam for their pupils to sing or play. Instrumental music is, in any case, very much influenced by vocal music.

When a singer sings the note *ma tivra* (sharpened *ma*), he or she would still sing the word 'ma', and *ni komal* would still be sung as 'ni'. But when written down, a tivra note would be written with a short line above the letter, and a komal note with a short line below. For example:

M̄ = ma tivra   N̠ = ni komal

Simple rhythms also can be notated within the sargam system. Each beat is called a *mātrā*, and curved lines are placed under the sargam letters to show which notes are grouped together within a single beat. More complex rhythm patterns must be memorized.

S R R G   P D D S   S D P   P PDP G R   G R   S R G P G R S

Assignment 56   Take C as *sa*. Play this melody from Indian notation:

S S | R GG M M | P P P MM | P Ṡ̇ Ṡ̇ N̠ D | P M G PP | M GG R S R | S

Assignment 57   Make up a short melody and write it in sargam. Sing it, or play it on an instrument. Exchange your melodies with other class members, and sing or play through each other's sargam melodies.

Ragas

Most Western music is based on the major and minor scales, and the pattern of intervals between the notes of each scale is always the same. Western musicians have to learn which sharps or flats are needed in the key signature of each scale to make it sound correct.

Indian music is based on *ragas*. A raga is not simply a scale. It is a cross between a scale and a melody. Each raga has very strict rules about which notes may be used, and *how* they may be used. Even the decorations and grace notes, which are an important part of Indian classical music, must be played in accordance with the rules of the raga. Decorations help to set the mood which each raga has to express.

All ragas are associated with a particular time of day or night when they should be performed, and many are named after gods and goddesses, and express their temperaments and characteristics.

Some ragas vary in ascent and descent, in rather the same way that the Western melodic minor scale varies in ascent and descent.

D melodic minor

Raga Khamaj (*Sa* = D)

Indian classical music is not written down for performance purposes. Musicians must memorize the ragas, and the moods and characteristics which they express. Each raga has certain important notes and phrases which must be emphasized during an improvisation.

The traditional way of performing a raga is in three sections:

1 **Alap** In this section the main artist, backed by the tamburā drone, slowly explores the notes of the raga with free improvisation.
2 **Jhor** This section is slightly faster, and has more of a pulse.
3 **Jhala** This is when the tablā player joins in, and the musicians improvise in both rhythm and melody. This section is usually fast and exciting, with the musicians passing rhythmic ideas back and forth to each other in their improvisations.

Assignment 58
CD TRACK 23

Listen to the opening of a performance by Hariprasad Chaurasia (flute) of raga Manjh Khamaj, an evening raga. There is a second flute part, used as an additional accompaniment. Quite often, accompanying parts are provided by students of the main performer. Describe the music played by the accompanying flute, and compare it with Hariprasad Chaurasia's part.

Here are some ragas, set out as ascending and descending scales. In each case, *sa* is D:

Raga Bhupali

Raga Khamaj

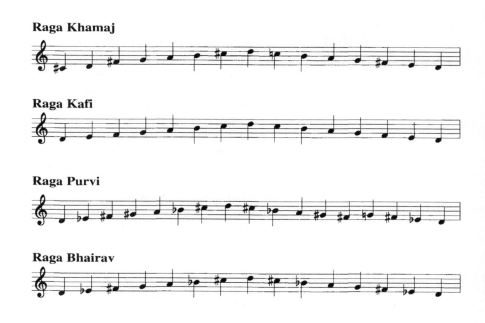

Raga Kafi

Raga Purvi

Raga Bhairav

Assignment 59　Play through these raga-scales. Make up a melody in the one you like best, and have a partner play a tamburā drone for you on a re-tuned guitar.

Hariprasad Chaurasia (flute) in concert with Mr Gopalkrishnan (violin)

39

Talas – rhythmic cycles

There are over 300 different talas, or rhythmic cycles, in Indian music, and like the ragas they all have names. However, some are used more frequently than others. Indian musicians must have a thorough knowledge of talas when they improvise, so that their playing has rhythmic structure. They must play the first beat of each cycle together with the tablā player, even though they may pass through very complex individual improvisations during the rest of the cycle.

Each tala has a certain number of beats, or mātrās, per cycle. And each cycle is divided into a number of sections, called *vibhāgs*.

The first beat of any tala is called the *sam*. It is very important that in every improvisation the performers must be together at each *sam*, and the piece must end on a *sam*.

In every tala there is one vibhāg (sometimes two) which must form a contrast. These contrasting vibhāgs are called *khālī*, which literally means 'empty'. When the tala is played on a pair of tablā, the khālī vibhāgs are played on the smaller drum only, while both drums are used for the other vibhāgs.

By far the most popular tala is *tīn-tāl* (sometimes written *teental*). This has 16 beats per cycle, divided into four equal vibhāgs.

1	2	3	4	5	6	7	8	9	10	11	12	13	14	15	16
X				X				0				X			

Each X indicates where to clap, and the 0 indicates a khālī vibhāg. The first beat is *sam*, and in tīn-tāl, as you can see, the third vibhāg of each cycle is a khālī vibhāg.

When Indian musicians clap tīn-tāl, they go through a set pattern of movements. For the first vibhāg, they clap the first beat, then place the 2nd, 3rd and 4th fingers of the right hand, in turn, against the left palm. The second and fourth vibhāgs are treated in exactly the same way. Try it.

The third khālī vibhāg goes like this. On the first beat (beat 9), place the back of your right hand against the palm of the left, then for beats 10–12 curl the fingers of the left, one at a time, around the right.

Assignment 60
CD TRACK 24

Practise clapping tīn-tāl as described, and then clap it along with the CD. (You will hear clapping on the CD to help you.) Now clap along with these other talas in the same way. There will always be clapping on the CD to help you.

CD TRACK 25

Ek-tāl

1	2	3	4	5	6	7	8	9	10	11	12
X		0		X		0		X		X	

CD TRACK 26

Kehrva

1	2	3	4
X		0	

Jhap-tāl

1	2	3	4	5	6	7	8	9	10
X		X			0		X		

Rūpak-tāl

1	2	3	4	5	6	7
0			X		X	

Dādrā

1	2	3	4	5	6
X			0		

Dhamār

1	2	3	4	5	6	7	8	9	10	11	12	13	14
X					X		0			X			

Assignment 61

Tablā player, Nilesh Rupani

Get into pairs, or small groups. One person claps the tala, while any others improvise rhythm patterns to go with it, using percussion instruments. Always play the *sam* together, and use contrasting sounds for the khālī vibhāg.

Playing the tablā

Before a tablā player learns to improvise, he or she must learn to make the great variety of sounds which can be produced with various combinations of hands and fingers on the two drums. The tablā player must know the names of all the strokes; these are called *bols*, which literally means 'words'.

Look at the diagram of a pair of tablā, as seen from above. The round black patch on each drum is called the *duggi*, and is made from a paste of rice flour and iron filings.

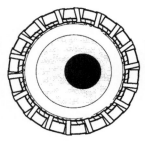

bāyā　　　　*dāyā*

Here are some of the strokes for the left hand:

gi gi   2nd and 3rd fingertips strike the bāyā. Pressure on the wrist can raise the pitch of the drum, giving it a range of an octave when played by a skilful performer.

ki   The flat hand strikes the bāyā with the wrist resting on the drum.

kat   The flat hand strikes the bāyā like a slap.

Here are some strokes for the right hand:

ti ta   The 2nd and 3rd fingertips strike the duggi firmly.

na   The 2nd finger strikes along the rim.

tin   The skin is struck between the rim and the duggi in a brushing movement.

And here are some strokes for both hands:

   na + gi = dha
   tin + gi = dhin
   ti ta + gi = dhita

There are many more bols than these!

Assignment 62
CD TRACK 31

Listen to the recording of all these different strokes, and the sound they make, while reading through the descriptions above. Each type of stroke is first played at a slow tempo, and then several more times, each at double the speed. You will have to listen carefully as they follow each other without a pause.

Assignment 63
CD TRACK 32

Listen to this performance by Vijay Kangutkar. As he speeds up, you will hear him recite the bols he intends to play, very fast, and then play them. This is a technique often used by expert tablā players to demonstrate their skill.

Notice the harmonium accompaniment, which is called a *laharā*. It is there to give a repeated phrase of melody which fits the tala, and give the solo tablā player something on which to base his improvisations. This only happens when the tablā player is the soloist, as opposed to when he is accompanying another performer, such as a sitar or sarod player.

There are set laharā for each tala. Here is the one being used for this tīn-tāl demonstration:

Assignment 64   Play through this laharā using a keyboard (or harmonium). If the pitch matches, you could try playing it with the CD (track 32).(Many keyboards include a pitch adjuster, so you can make sure you are in tune with the CD.)

Assignment 65   Try playing some of the tablā strokes yourself, following the descriptions on the previous page. If you have no access to a set of tablā, you can get the feel of playing them by using bongo or conga drums, but the sound will not be like that of the tablā. Why not?

Other Indian drums

Many other types of drums are used widely in India for folk and dance music, religious music, and popular music. There is also a variety of other percussion instruments.

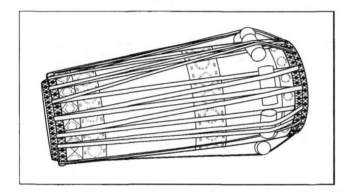

The *pakhāvaj* is a large wooden cylindrical drum with a playing membrane at both ends, one of which is larger than the other. It is played by the hands, one at each end of the drum, using palms and fingers to produce a variety of strokes in much the same way that a tablā player executes the various bols.

The *mṛdaṅgam* (right) is the most important south Indian drum. It is used for classical music, like the north Indian tablā. The mṛdaṅgam is made from a hollowed block of wood. The left membrane has a circle of flour paste applied to it, which gives a bass sound. The right-hand surface has a circle of a mixture of manganese dust and iron filings with paste, to give resonance.

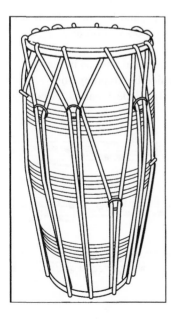

The *ḍholak* (left) is another wooden cylindrical drum with the membrane on one side larger than the other. It, too, is played with both hands, but is used more often for folk-music, particularly in the Punjab. The membranes are tuned by means of thick cords passed through metal rings around the sides of the drum.

43

Folk-music

India is a vast country with many languages. The country includes lush hills, rugged mountains, deserts, flat plains, and huge crowded cities, as well as thousands of small villages. The folk-music reflects the great variety of lifestyles and cultures. Like folk-music all over the world, it preserves local traditions and gives people a sense of belonging, as well as being an important part of the social life. We can only look at a few examples from various parts of India.

This is *Bamboo Dance* from Nagaland, in north-east India, near Assam. It is a dance performed by a group of young men. Some of the men hold long bamboo poles at each end, making patterns with them, while others jump on and over the poles. The dance gets more and more athletic and exciting as it goes on.

Assignment 66

Play *Bamboo Dance* in groups, starting with a few instruments and gradually adding more with every repeat of the melody to express the building excitement of the dance. The last verses should have plenty of rhythmic percussion.

The Punjab is known for its lively folk-music and dances, and it is from this area that *bhangra* originates – the type of pop music which has a great following among young Indians all over the world. Bhangra has been influenced in the UK by electronic instruments, the Western drum kit, and by styles such as 'rap'.

Assignment 67
CD TRACKS 33 AND 34

Listen to this famous bhangra song, 'Hey Jamalo' – first in its more traditional form as performed by Golden Star, and then in its 'remix' version by Bally Sagoo. Compare the two versions, and list the instruments used and also any other differences. Which version do you prefer?

Most folk-music from the Indian sub-continent is vocal and, as in many other parts of the world, much of it is accompanied by clapping and percussion. Here is the melody of a song from Bangladesh called 'Allah Megde', asking God to send rain.

Assignment 68   Play the melody of 'Allah Megde' on any suitable combination of instruments. How many different melodic phrases are there in this song?

Assignment 69
CD TRACK 35   Listen to this instrumental version of a fisherman's song from Bengal. The instrument you can hear playing a glissando scale is the *swaramandel*, a string instrument shaped like an oblong box with the strings tuned to a raga. It is stroked in this way to add atmosphere, and is often used by singers.
1   Which instrument plays the main tune?
2   Which instrument plays a drone?
3   What does the sitar play?
4   What other instruments can you hear?
5   Although there are no words in this version, how would you describe the mood?

Religious music

There are many religions practised in India, but the religion with the greatest number of followers is Hinduism. There are special songs and chants used in Hindu temples, and music is greatly revered.

Some of the chants are led by a *swami* (priest or leader) with the congregation joining in alternate phrases, rather like the responses in a Christian church. These are called *bhajans*. You may have heard one of these, especially if you have been to London and heard members of the Radha Krishna Temple chanting in the streets. Their most famous chant is called 'Hare Krishna, Hare Rama', and is sung in praise of the gods Krishna and Rama.

A minstrel, with his ancient folk fiddle, stands near an age-old religious figure and sings his traditional songs which, also, are hundreds of years old

45

The *arti* is another type of Hindu religious song concerning gods and goddesses. Here is the melody of 'Ragu Pati', which was said to be a favourite of the great Indian leader Mahatma Gandhi, who lived from 1869 to 1948. (Ragu Pati is another name for the Hindu god, Rama.)

Assignment 70

Play through this melody, and the one on the previous page, using instruments in a way which might imitate how they would be sung.

Muslims have a form of religious chanting called *qawwālī*. The chants are performed by men, one or two lead singers alternating with the rest of the group. The other men in the group clap rhythmically and sing the responses to the accompaniment of tablā and harmonium. This is yet another example of call-and-response.

Assignment 71
CD TRACK 36

Listen to this recording of 'Allah Hoo Allah Hoo Allah Hoo' (Praise God) by Ustād Nusrat Fateh Ali Khan and party. Clap along softly with the CD.

Film music

The Indian film industry is one of the largest in the world, and nearly all the films include music and dance. During recent years the film music has been influenced by Western rock and pop music, but music from earlier films is still very popular with people of all age groups.

Songs are not usually sung by the actors and actresses, but by 'playback' singers whose voices are recorded so that the film stars can mime the songs. The playback singers become equally famous – even though their faces never appear on the screen – and they tour India and other countries, giving concerts.

Assignment 72

Try to obtain recordings by some of the famous 'playback' singers – for instance Lata Mangeshkar or Asha Bhosle – and listen to them. Notice the sounds and instruments you hear, and the musical styles, and describe how they contribute to the whole effect of the songs. Do you like this music?

'Playback' singer, Asha Bhosle

46

The gamelan music of Indonesia

Gamelan is the general term used for a set of musical instruments consisting of tuned gongs and metallophones. There are three different gamelan cultures in Indonesia, based in Central Java, Western Java (Sunda), and Bali. Although there are differences in musical style between the three, they have all developed from the same tradition.

Assignment 73
CD TRACK 37

Listen to this piece of Balinese gamelan music, an extract from *Tabuh Loma-Loma* recorded at the temple of Batur. (The Balinese word *tabuh* means 'to strike', and also 'ostinato'.) Pick out the most important melody and quietly sing it with the recording. How many different notes can you find in the melody?

The Indonesian islands have had trade links with China and India for two thousand years. There have been many invasions and migrations, all of which have had an effect on the religion, language, government and art-forms of Indonesia.

In the fifth century, Hinduism was brought to Bali and Java, and Hindu documents tell of a very active musical life amongst poor as well as rich people. It is known from temple carvings and pictures that all the types of gamelan instruments used today were in use by the sixteenth century.

With the Muslim invasion, Islam spread through Java during the fifteenth century. Many Hindu princes fled to Bali with their courts, complete with musicians, dancers, actors and artists. To this day Bali is mainly Hindu; and Java mainly Muslim. In Bali, the Hindu religion features strongly in all art-forms, and the stories used for dance-dramas, accompanied by gamelan music, are very much based on Hindu mythology.

Balinese dance-drama

The sounds of the gamelan

The sound produced by a set of gamelan instruments is unique. Many of the instruments have a rather similar sound quality, or timbre, and so it is not very easy for the inexperienced listener to work out how the complex texture of sound is being achieved. This will become clearer later when we examine each type of instrument and the music it plays.

Assignment 74
CD TRACK 38

Listen to this piece of music, an extract from *Tabuh Pisan*, recorded at the temple of Tampaksiring, Bali.

1 Can you hear a main tune?
2 Is there another type of instrument playing the main tune with the metallophones?
3 Is there any harmonic accompaniment, in the sense of a changing sequence of chords?
4 Is there an independent bass part which moves in contrary motion to the main tune?
5 In this particular extract is there any contrast between loud and soft passages?

Gamelan scales

Gamelan music is based on two main scales:

1 *Slendro* (Central Javanese and Balinese name) or *salendro* (Sundanese name)
2 *Pelog*

Slendro is a five-note scale, and is considered to be an attempt to divide the octave into five equal intervals. The tuning of sets of gamelan instruments varies, so it is not possible to write gamelan music in Western notation, but slendro sounds similar to any of these Western-notated versions:

When gamelan melodies are written down, they are written in numbers. But the notes do have names, which are:

(Javanese names)	barang	gulu	dada	lima	nem
	1	2	3	4	5
(Balinese names)	ding	dong	deng	dung	dang

Assignment 75

Take a chromatic xylophone or glockenspiel (if possible one with notes that can be removed) and, by counting out the semitone intervals, work out a slendro scale with the intervals between the notes as equal as possible. You can use any note you choose as *barang*. Remove all the other notes and label your slendro scale using the Javanese or Balinese names, whichever you prefer. Improvise some short melodies.

Assignment 76

Collect six of the largest glass bottles you can find, and tap them gently with a xylophone beater. Put water in the one that makes the lowest sound when empty. Put enough water in it to make the lowest note possible. This becomes *barang*. Now find another bottle which, with or without water, makes a note an octave higher; this note is called *barang alit*. Try hard to ignore what you are used to hearing as the Western scale and, by filling the bottles to the correct levels with water, tune them to five equidistant intervals. Now you have your own individual slendro scale. Play some of the melodies which you made up in the previous assignment.

The pelog scale has seven notes, which are not at all equidistant. The names of the pelog scale are:

(Java & Bali)	bem	gulu	dada	pelog	lima	nem	barang
	1	2	3	4	5	6	7
(Sunda)	singul	galimer	penelu	bungur	loloran	nem	barang

Pelog scales vary. Here is the nearest Western equivalent to one found in Sunda, and to one found in Java.

Assignment 77   Using a xylophone or glockenspiel, invent your own pelog scale. What do you notice about the first interval in both scales quoted in assignment 76? This is quite usual, so you could incorporate it into your scale. Improvise some tunes.

Sets of gamelan instruments which are tuned for both slendro *and* pelog are called double gamelan. The sets of notes for the two scales are laid out at right angles. However, many sets are tuned just for one scale or the other.

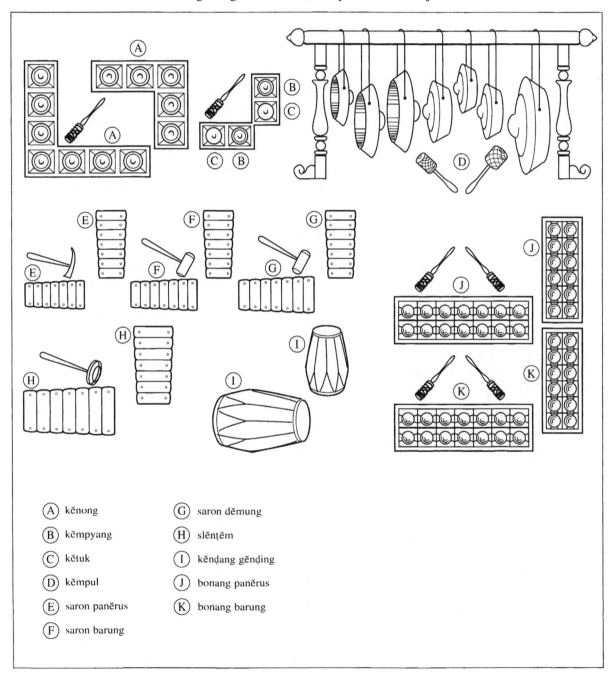

(A) kĕnong

(B) kĕmpyang

(C) kĕtuk

(D) kĕmpul

(E) saron panĕrus

(F) saron barung

(G) saron dĕmung

(H) slĕnṭĕm

(I) kĕnḍang gĕnḍing

(J) bonang panĕrus

(K) bonang barung

How a double gamelan is set out

The gamelan instruments and the music they play

Each piece of gamelan music is based on a main tune, sometimes called the principal melody, or the nuclear theme. All the melody instruments play either the whole theme, or parts of the theme, or variations on the theme. The instruments can be divided into groups according to the part they play in the whole performance. In addition, there are rhythm instruments, and instruments which mark the ends of the sections and phrases.

Group 1: Balungan instruments

These play the nuclear theme, called the *balungan*. They include the *saron* family. These are single-octave metallophones which have heavy bronze keys with a hole at each end, which slot onto pins on a wooden trough. In poorer villages, the keys may be made of iron or brass. Sarons are played with a wooden mallet held in the right hand, while the left hand damps the notes to stop them echoing and blurring the tune. *Saron panĕrus* is the high octave saron, which plays each note of the tune twice. *Saron barung* (middle octave) and *saron dĕmung* (low octave) play the nuclear theme in a straightforward way.

An octave below the saron demung is the *slĕnţĕm*, which often plays the notes of the nuclear theme leaving out the fourth beat of each measure. It is the only single-octave member of the *gĕnder* family (pronounced 'gendere' with a 'soft' g) which will be described later.

saron

Group 2: Interpunctuating instruments

The nuclear theme is divided into phrases by various instruments of the gong family. The larger gongs are suspended vertically on a wooden frame. They are made of bronze and have a bump in the centre known as the *boss*. This is struck with a large padded stick. The largest gong is the *gong agĕng*, which may be up to a metre in diameter and weigh 68kg (150lbs).

The *kĕnong* are smaller gongs which rest horizontally on cords strung across box frames. They are struck with hollow sticks wound round with twine at the ends.

The *kĕmpyang* is a pair of small, high-pitched horizontal gongs. The *kĕtuk* (pronounced 'k'tuk') is a pair of flatter gongs which have a sound that is immediately damped. Its name describes its sound – k'tuk.

Gamelan music is divided into measures of four beats. Each group of four beats is called a *keteg*, and is rather like a bar in Western music. However, in gamelan music the fourth beat of the keteg is considered to be the strongest, whereas in Western music the first beat is the strongest.

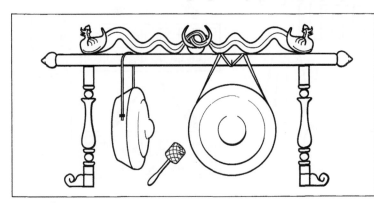

gong agĕng

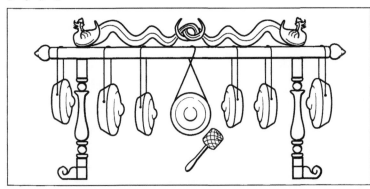

kĕmpul – medium-sized gongs

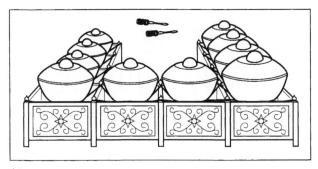

kĕnong

kĕmpyang

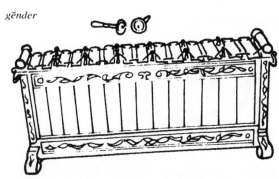

kĕtuk

The following diagram gives an idea of how some of the interpunctuating instruments divide up the music. A complete rhythmic cycle is called a *gongan*. The first gong and kĕnong sound in the diagram is really the last beat of the previous gongan.

	keteg	2	3	4	5	6	7	8	9	10	11	12	13	14	15	16
gong	X															X
kĕnong	X				X				X				X			X
kĕtuk		X		X		X		X		X		X		X		
kĕmpul			X				X				X				X	

*(spanning header above: **gongan**)*

Group 3: Panerusan instruments

The purpose of the instruments of this group is to play a melody based on decorations and embellishments of the nuclear theme.

gĕnder

The gĕnder family has thin bronze keys suspended in a frame over bamboo resonators which hang down rather like the resonators on an orchestral xylophone. A disc-headed stick is held in each hand, and the keys are damped by the thumbs. Each gĕnder, except the slĕnțĕm mentioned earlier, has a range of two-and-a-half octaves. *Gĕnder panĕrus* is the highest, and *gĕnder barung* is an octave lower.

51

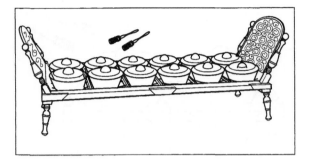

bonang

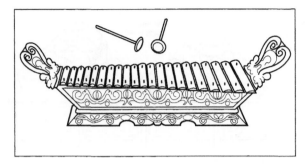

gambang

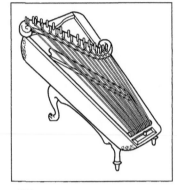

cĕlĕmpung

The *bonang* family consists of two sets of gong-chimes (sets of knobbed gong kettles), each with a range of two octaves. The gong kettles rest on crossed cords stretched across a single frame. *Bonang panĕrus* sounds an octave higher than *bonang barung*. They are played with padded sticks.

Other instruments are also sometimes included in this group. *Gambang kayu* is a wooden-keyed xylophone with a three-and-a-half octave range and a more mellow sound than the Western xylophone. The *cĕlĕmpung* is a type of 14-string zither with strings stretched across a box shape plucked with the thumbnails.

The *rabāb* is a two-string instrument played with a bow. It is of Persian or Arabian origin. In softer pieces it plays a more elaborate version of the melody, still based on the nuclear theme.

The *suling*, an end-blown flute, is frequently used in gamelan music, and there are occasions when a female singer, and a chorus of male singers, also perform.

Assignment 78
CD TRACKS 39 AND 40

Listen to a short extract from a much longer performance of Javanese gamelan music, played in slendro scale. There is a slow-moving, gentle effect, and the piece is sung in an old Javanese poetic language.

Then listen to an extract from *Gĕnding Anglirmendung* – traditional Javanese music, played in pelog scale, used to accompany the slow, stylized movements of the classical *Serimpi* court dance.

Describe the musical texture of each of these pieces. Which instruments, as far as you can hear, are performing which function within the texture?

Group 4: Rhythm instruments
The most important of the rhythm instruments are the *kĕndang gĕnding*, and the *kĕtipung*. Both are conical drums with one end larger than the other, and a playing skin at each end. They are played with both hands, but the kĕtipung is considerably smaller. These drums play sounds which are

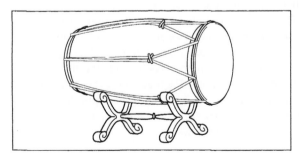

kĕndang gĕnding (left) and kĕtipung (below)

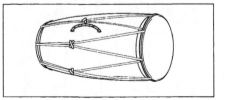

bĕḍug

indicated by words, in much the same way as the tablā players of India play tablā bols. (Remember that 'bols' means 'words' in Hindi.) The kĕnḍang 'bols' are called *kĕnḍangans*.

The function of these drums is to cue in the orchestra, indicate the tempo, and accent the movements of dancers or puppets.

Some other percussion instruments are also sometimes used:

1 The *bĕḍug* – a large barrel-shaped drum beaten with sticks
2 *Kĕprak* – wood blocks
3 *Kĕkrek* – metal plates
4 *Kĕcer* (pronounced 'keshere') – small cymbals

Notice how most of the names of Indonesian instruments describe the sounds they make. For example, 'keshere' sounds like the echo produced when a cymbal is clashed, 'kĕprak' sounds like the crack of wood blocks and 'gong agĕng' sounds like the ring and echo of a large gong.

Assignment 79   Look back at the descriptions of the Indonesian instruments and think of some new names for Western instruments which describe the sounds they make.

Some of the instruments in a Balinese gamelan accompanying a trance dance

Do-it-yourself gamelan

Assignment 80
CD TRACK 41

Here is the score of a piece of music from Bali called *Rearing Horse* which is arranged for gamelan instruments. You can hear the piece on the accompanying CD, performed on an electronic keyboard. (It was recorded by superimposing the parts one by one.)

Listen to the recording, and follow the music.

Then try to reproduce this piece using electronic keyboards, xylophones, glockenspiels or any other suitable instruments which are available.

First, work out which instrument or keyboard voice would be suitable for each of the parts. To do this you may need to look back at the instrument descriptions. You will notice that the melody of each part has a fairly narrow note range but, in some cases, a tricky rhythm. So practise each part slowly and carefully before getting together in a group to play the complete piece.

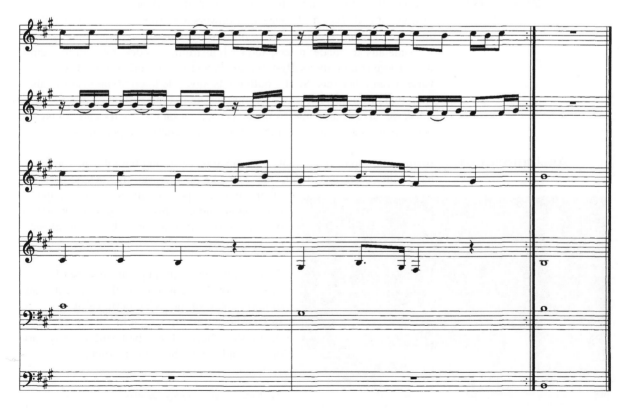

The social nature of gamelan performance

Gamelan music expresses the deepest beliefs and feelings of the Indonesian people. Their culture does not permit open displays of emotion, but through gamelan music they can express themselves – not only when listening or participating, but also when gamelan is used as part of other art-forms such as dance, drama, poetry performances and shadow puppet plays.

Gamelan music is associated with all celebrations and rituals of birth, marriage and death, as well as natural and religious festivals – just as songs are used for these events in other cultures.

In villages, the gamelan is often housed in an open-sided square pavilion, which is the centre for the social and festive occasions of the village community. The gamelan is performed at all these events.

Gamelan music has always played an important part in court and state ceremony, as a means of celebration as well as for entertainment. Court gamelans are very ornate and cast in bronze, but village gamelans are simpler and made of iron or brass, and bamboo.

Traditionally gamelans are played by men and boys, but more recently all-female groups began to form. However, mixed groups are still unusual in Indonesia. Gamelan musicians play together as a group, and there are no 'star' players who perform as individuals. The music is presented as a whole, as if from one large instrument, requiring many players. Musicians are trained to play all the instruments, learning mostly by imitation and memorization.

Respect for the gamelan

Gamelan instruments are always treated with great respect, as it is believed that they have spiritual powers. Indonesian people never step over an instrument, as they believe this would break the link between the instrument and Heaven. Incense and flowers are offered to sets of gamelan, and name-giving ceremonies take place when a new gamelan is made.

Gamelans are made in sets, and each instrument is decorated in the same way. There is no universally-fixed pitch, and so the tuning of each set varies from other sets. So it would not be possible to combine instruments from two different sets, as they would not be in tune with each other.

As we have seen, gamelan music is used for dance, poetry and drama performances as well as for the very popular shadow puppet plays.

Assignment 81

In groups of up to five, create a gamelan piece. Using the information you have gathered earlier in this chapter, make up a nuclear theme, add parts for other gamelan-type instruments, and also add percussion, and perhaps a suling part. Decide on a mood or part of a story which your music could express.

Gamelan music is still popular, in spite of the influence of Western 'pop' in the cities. It is an important part of the living heritage of Indonesia, and is still taught in the schools and the music colleges. It can be heard at every sort of celebration and theatre performance.

Students learning to play gamelan

The music of China

Ancient traditions

The Chinese civilization is amongst the oldest in the world, and a musical system and musical instruments were developed in China long before most other countries. The ancient Chinese believed that music could influence people's souls, and affect the world of nature and natural phenomena. When the notes of the musical scale were fixed, they were associated with the planets and with the months of the year. Religious chants and songs had to start on a certain note of the scale, according to the month in which the ceremony took place.

Music was always inspired by nature, and descriptive music has always been popular in China, from ancient times to the present day.

Assignment 82
CD TRACK 42

Listen to this piece called *Chinese Martial Arts*. Does this music conjure up a picture in your imagination? How is this effect achieved?

At the time of the Emperor Fuh Shi, around 3000 BC, a system of music had already been developed, and many musical instruments had been invented. These included types of lute, lyre, and a stringed zither which was the predecessor of the *ch'in*, still in use today. In 2633 BC the ch'in had five strings, which represented the five planets then known: Mercury, Venus, Mars, Jupiter and Saturn. The ch'in now has seven strings.

Music for the ch'in is very complicated, as players have to read characters telling them which string to use, which finger to use, and how the note is to be played. The strings are now tuned to the notes G, A, C, D, E, G, A – a pentatonic scale.

Assignment 83
CD TRACK 43

Listen to this ch'in music which is called *Liushui* (Flowing waters). Does this music 'paint a picture' as effectively as the piece you heard earlier? Do you think that the pitch-range of this instrument is wide, medium, or narrow? Listen carefully for the lowest and highest notes that you can hear.

Playing the ch'in

The story of the Chinese scale

It was around 2679 BC, at the time of the Emperor Huang Ti (whose name means 'Yellow Emperor'), that the pitch of a root bass was fixed and called *Huang-chung* (Yellow Bell) The twelve notes of the octave were also fixed, and named. There are several slightly different versions of how this was done, but all end with the same result – and the gist of the story is this:

A man called Ling Lun (whose name means 'Ruler of Music') went to a valley full of tall bamboo. He cut a length of hollow bamboo and blew through it to fix the fundamental bass note. He then chose lengths of bamboo of the same thickness and diameter and made a set of pitchpipes.

Let us say that the pitch of the fundamental bass was C. It probably was not, and we will never know exactly what it was, but choosing C makes the principle easier to explain.

The ancient Chinese number-symbol for Heaven was three, and for Earth was two. So, dividing the length of the fundamental into three, and cutting the next pipe two-thirds the length of the fundamental, produces the note a perfect 5th higher than the fundamental – G. The Chinese feel that the interval of a perfect 5th is the most harmonious. The next note, D, was produced by cutting a pipe two-thirds the length of G. However, this would have produced a note outside the octave C to C. So the length of the D tube was doubled to produce the D one octave lower.

All the other notes were each produced from the previous note in the same way, and whenever the newly-generated note was outside the C to C octave, the pipe length was doubled to produce the note an octave lower.

The twelve resultant pitches were called *lü*. Here they are, in Western notation:

The twelve lü were associated with the months of the year, and for many centuries the chanting for religious ceremonies had to begin on the lü associated with the particular month. Although twelve notes were found, there is no such thing as a chromatic scale in Chinese music. The first five notes were the only ones used for many centuries – although the sound of this scale could be transposed to any pitch, so that the melodies and chants could begin on any lü in rather the same way that Western music has different keys.

The first five lü form the pentatonic scale. The Chinese consider music based on these notes to be the most harmonious, as there are no semitones, and so it is easier to sing. (This is probably why many folk-songs all over the world are composed in the pentatonic scale.)

At the top of the next page you can see a diagram showing the construction of the pitchpipes, the names of the lü, what they mean, and the months and hours to which they correspond. Notice that the first five most-used pipes also had a second, shorter name.

Huang-chung	Lin-chung	T'ai-ts'u	Nan-lü	Ku-hsien	Ying-chung	Jui-pin	Ta-lü	I-tse	Chia-chung	Wu-i	Chung-lü
Yellow Bell	Forest Bell	Great Frame	Southern Tube	Old Pure	Answer-ing Bell	Luxuriant Vegeta-tion	Greatest Tube	Equaliz-ing Rule	Pressed Bell	Not Ter-minated	Mean Tube
11th moon 11th hour	6th moon 1st hour	1st moon 3rd hour	8th moon 5th hour	3rd moon 7th hour	10th moon 9th hour	5th moon 11th hour	12th moon 1st hour	7th moon 3rd hour	2nd moon 5th hour	9th moon 7th hour	4th moon 9th hour
Kung	Chih	Shang	Yü	Chüeh							
King	Affairs of the country	Ministers	Natural world	People							

Assignment 84

It is possible to make a set of pitchpipes from narrow plastic tube (2cm diameter). This is used for plumbing, and can be bought in 2-metre lengths from most DIY shops. Two such lengths will be needed. The tubing is easy to cut with a sharp knife – but be careful. Cut with the sharp side of the blade facing away from you, and with the tube resting on a hard surface.

1 Cut a length 27 inches long to make the fundamental, *Huang-chung* (Yellow Bell) (alternative shorter name, *Kung*).
2 Two-thirds of 27 = 18. Therefore cut a length 18 inches long to make *Lin-chung* (Forest Bell) (*Chih*).
3 Two-thirds of 18 = 12. Double it to 24 inches, and cut that length to make *T'ai-ts'u* (*Shang*).
4 Two-thirds of 24 = 16. Cut a length 16 inches to make *Nan-lü* (*Yü*).
5 Two-thirds of 16 = $10^2/3$. Double it to $21^1/3$ inches and cut that length to make *Ku-hsien* (*Chüeh*).

Please note that these tube lengths will not give you the sound of C, D, E, G and A. In fact my 27-inch 'Yellow Bell' fundamental tube sounds the B below middle C. These lengths were chosen to make the arithmetic easier. If you calculate in centimetres you could start with 81 cm as your fundamental tube – but with a longer fundamental tube you will use a lot more plastic tube.

Assignment 85   You have just made a set of one-note flutes. Let each one be played by a different person. Blow across the top, as if you were blowing a flute, to produce the sound. Now blow across the top again but with the flat of your hand blocking off the other end of the tube. What happens?

Now combine your efforts to improvise some melodies using all the notes you can produce.

Language, melody and notation

All speech has an element of music in it, as the voice naturally rises and falls and the words make rhythm patterns. This is particularly true of the Chinese language, which is largely monosyllabic. There are many words which are pronounced in a similar way to each other, but the intonation of the voice makes all the difference. In Chinese, the characters in which the language is written also express the rise and fall of the voice.

Chinese musical notation was written using the same characters as the words – the sign meant the pitch as well as the note-name.

During the Yuan Dynasty, AD 1279–1368, the Mongols invaded China led by Kublai Khan, grandson of the mighty warrior, Genghis Khan. The Mongols brought with them a different scale and notation system. The scale was similar to the Western major scale, and their system of writing notes was simpler than the Chinese and soon became more popular. Both Chinese and Mongol characters are read from top to bottom of the page, and in columns arranged from right to left.

There is no universal way of writing rhythm, so Chinese musicians could only get a rough idea of the piece by reading the pitch. They had to hear it performed to learn it properly. Four-time is nearly always used, and the bar endings are shown by a small circle next to the character.

Nowadays, Chinese musicians often play from Western notation, and sometimes from numbers or characters.

Chinese music is very much based on melody. Until the influence of Western music reached China, at the beginning of the century, there was no chordal harmony or counterpoint. As in several of the other cultures we have studied, musicians played heterophonically. In other words, each musician would play his or her version of the melody, adding decorations and variations of pace as suitable.

Here is the melody of a song about a wife searching for her husband, who has been forced into a labour gang to build the Great Wall of China. The wall was built in an attempt to keep out the Mongol invaders in the Chin Dynasty (221–206 BC).

Assignment 86   Play through this melody on any instrument. What type of scale is being used? What do you notice about the range of notes used in this tune compared with, for example, Arab music?

Now form a group of three or four and play the tune again, each of you varying and embellishing the tune, so that you are playing heterophonically.

There is a huge variety of Chinese musical instruments, many of them unlike any instrument found in the West – for example, stone chimes, originally made of jade and used for ceremonial music.

There are huge instruments for use in temples, such as drums with a diameter of six feet or more. Instruments were very important to temple ceremonies, and were used in large numbers.

Here is a ceremonial chant in honour of Confucius, called *The Guiding March*. The dots over the notes indicate where percussion instruments are to be played.

sheng

J. A. Van Aalst, who worked in the Imperial Customs Service at the end of the last century, described the orchestra which played *The Guiding March* as being made up of two of each of the following instruments:

Hsiao – a type of flute, end-blown, with a hole at the back and five holes in the front.

Ti-tzu – a side-blown flute.

Tou-kuan – a bamboo pipe with a reed at one end, similar in sound to an oboe.

Yün-lo – a vertically-held glockenspiel type of instrument with ten gongs, of different sizes and pitches, hung from a frame. The name means 'cloud-gong'.

Sheng – a type of mouth organ which might have 13, 15, 17 or 19 pipes, pushed into an earthenware pot, forming a circular air chamber.

Drums and castanets.

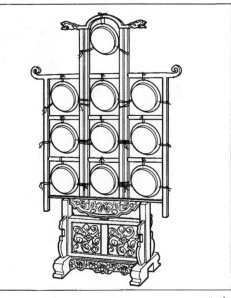

yün-lo

Assignment 87

Play *The Guiding March*, using whatever instruments you can find which give a similar sound to those described. Write out the percussion part in notation, including rests. Do you think the castanets would have played exactly the same as the drummers? Use your imagination and invent some variations, while keeping to the basic idea of the original.

Sounds of Chinese instruments

During the Tang Dynasty (AD 618–907) instrumental music at court was very highly developed. Emperor Ming Hoang was a composer and would join in with the palace orchestral performances. History tells of one festival which involved 10,000 musicians, divided into nine groups, and playing 300 different types of instruments.

An 'ordinary' Imperial orchestra would consist of a conductor, several sets of stone chimes, over 100 harps, 50 lutes, 200 sheng, 20 tou-kuan, and 200 guitar-type instruments (*pipas* or *yüeh-ch'in*). When you consider that these instruments would have been played heterophonically, it must have been an amazing sound!

Assignment 88
CD TRACKS 44 AND 45

Listen to part of *Himalayas*, played by the Guo Brothers. It features the *dizi*, a bamboo flute, with sheng and percussion accompaniment.

And listen to part of *Han Palace by Autumn Moonlight*, which features the *erh-hu*, a two-string fiddle, along with an accompanying ensemble of various instruments.

For both tracks, describe briefly the characteristic sounds of the featured instruments, and also identify what other types of instruments you can hear.

Playing the erh-hu

East meets west

The Ching Dynasty came to an end in 1911 when China became a Republic. However, a period of turmoil and change had begun in 1840 with Western invasions and colonisation. The typical Chinese attitudes of humility and respect for tradition were no match for Western technology and aggression.

During the last years of the Ching Dynasty and the early years of the Republic, much of the old court music was regarded as inferior to the music of Western culture. A new type of Chinese music evolved incorporating some aspects of Western music. Gradually, both harmony and equal temperament were introduced, although the scale used was still largely pentatonic, or at most diatonic.

The design of musical instruments was improved to give a wider range of notes. Instruments began to be built in families – soprano, alto, tenor and bass – like Western instruments. Chinese orchestras and music colleges were set up. Orchestral music was often influenced by folk-music, and was usually descriptive, which is still true to this day.

Assignment 89
CD TRACKS 46 AND 47

Listen to *Dance Music of Hua T'iao Tzu*, and *Without a Song*. Both are based on folk-music. Compare and contrast the mood, instrumentation and musical texture of the pieces.

Nowadays Chinese music and musical instruments are taught in schools and colleges, but students are also interested in studying Western music.

Music, history and ideology

The great sage and philosopher Confucius lived from 551 to 479 BC during the Chou Dynasty. His thinking and writings have influenced every aspect of Chinese culture during the last two thousand years.

Around 200 BC, a set of books known as 'The Five Classics' were written, giving instructions in the principles of Confucius' teachings. These books included a music book called *Shi King*, or 'Book of Odes'. During the Chou Dynasty it was believed that music was a part of scientific knowledge, and that only someone with an understanding of music was fit to govern. An 'Office of Music' was created as a government department to ensure that musicians showed the officially approved attitudes of respect and humility, and that they kept to a standard pitch. Notice that the Chinese regarded standard pitch as important, unlike most other musical cultures.

Until this century, traditional attitudes of respect and humility were promoted by the well-educated emperors, courtiers and sages, and kept the poorer people 'in their places'. Music was an important part of court life.

In 1644, Manchurian rulers took over China, and there was a period of peace and prosperity in which the arts flourished.

Girls' ensemble performing yen-yüeh (court banquet music) in the reign of Emperor Hsüan-tsung (712–56) during the Tang Dynasty

People began to congregate towards the towns, and folk-music influenced court and festival music. Here is the melody of a song called 'Ching Ming' (Clear and bright) from Fukien Province in south-east China. It is the name of a spring festival in which people remember their ancestors.

Assignment 90

Play the melody of 'Ching Ming' in small groups using any suitable combination of instruments. Play it heterophonically, adding decorations and trills. Do not all necessarily play all the time. Arrange the piece to give variety. Add percussion instruments, too.

Throughout the dynasties, dating from China's earliest civilization, the power was held by the upper classes, the elite and the educated. This changed after the Civil War. The People's Republic of China was formed in 1949, led by Mao Tse-tung; the Nationalist Government, under Chiang Kai-shek, fled to the island of Taiwan. Under the new regime, workers and peasants were considered to be more important. The new music promoted and praised the revolutionary spirit. Composers and artists were treated as 'cultural workers', and had to undergo special training in socialist ideology, and to live amongst the people. Music was composed to praise workers and revolutionary heroes and heroines. There was also a revival of interest in Chinese instrumental music, and in regional folk-music and dramas.

Opera

Chinese opera has existed for centuries. The Peking Opera was founded during the seventeenth century and is still in operation today. In the early part of the Ching Dynasty, opera stories had to be about gods and goddesses, and anyone who produced an opera whose story did not meet with official approval was punished.

After the Civil War, eight revolutionary *yang-pan* model plays were composed, and performed by the Peking Opera. They were used to instruct people in the officially-approved attitudes, and these were the only operas that people were allowed to watch. The main characters were all larger-than-life revolutionary heroes and heroines.

For example, an opera called *Shachiapang* is set in a small town during the war of resistance against Japan. The hero, a political instructor, leads a group of wounded soldiers aided by Sister Ah-Ching, an underground worker of the Chinese Communist party. They plan counter-attacks and, after facing many difficulties, prevail in the end.

Chinese music today

Life was particularly strict during the period known as 'The Cultural Revolution', between 1966 and 1976. All Western music was banned, and so was any Chinese music based on Confucian ideals or any other religious traditions. After the death of Chairman Mao, however, and the fall of Madam Mao and the 'Gang of Four', music-theatre works other than the yang-pan plays were allowed to be produced and performed. The Chinese people were allowed to listen to a greater variety of music.

Since 1976, music from before the Cultural Revolution has been revived, including descriptive music such as the piece in the next assignment.

Assignment 91
CD TRACK 48

Listen to *Moonlight over Spring River*. Describe the types of instruments you can hear, even if you are not sure of their exact names.

This piece is very important in the history of Chinese music. Song words were composed during the seventh century, and the original melody dates from even earlier. It describes a boat drifting homewards in the moonlight. This piece of music is still popular. Can you think of any Western song which is still well known and quite popular after several hundred years? What is the oldest song you can find which would fit this description?

Folk-music and story-telling songs have also enjoyed a revival. But the newest form of music, heard on the mainland as well as in Hong Kong and Taiwan, is 'pop' music. Chinese pop music is a mixture of melodies using the typical Chinese scale (pentatonic) with the rhythms of rock, country and western, and various other styles.

Traditional characters in Chinese opera (left to right): old man, old woman, beautiful heroine, and scholar-lover

The music of Japan

Styles, traditions and influences

Japanese music, like most East Asian music cultures, tends to depend on words. Traditional Japanese music often has a vocal part, and the descriptive nature of instrumental music is usually reflected in the title.

Court orchestral music is very different from theatre music, but some characteristics apply to all traditional music:

1 There is no chordal harmony.
2 Melodic parts seem to start at different times, only coming together at cadences.
3 Japanese music tends to be 'through-composed', while Western music depends upon a more structured form in which there are answering phrases, variations and repeats, and a harmonic basis. Japanese music is a succession of new ideas, and although there is musical form, it does not depend on recognizable phrases being repeated.

The form of Japanese music falls under the headings *jo*, *ha*, and *kyū*: 'introduction', 'breaking away', and 'hurried'.

Assignment 92
CD TRACK 49

Listen to a piece by Mitzuhashi Koto called *Shochikubai* (Music of pine, bamboo and plum blossom) played on a *koto*, *shamisen*, and *kokyū*. The koto and shamisen are plucked string instruments, and the kokyū is bowed. Notice the features of the music mentioned above.

Western influence on technology has had a greater impact in Japan than in any other oriental country. Although there has been a rapid development in science and industry, there is a desire amongst the Japanese to preserve the traditional art-forms. In spite of the popularity of all types of Western music, whether classical or popular, traditional Japanese music is still highly respected. However, sometimes the style of performance is modified to suit modern audiences.

Assignment 93
CD TRACK 50

Listen to this descriptive music, *Nagare* (The stream), by the female composer Kazuko Tsukushi. It is played by kotos and *shakuhachi* (end-blown bamboo flute). Compared with the previous piece, do you think the performance style of this has been influenced by Western style? Give reasons for your opinion.

Playing the koto – the strings are plucked with ivory plectrums worn on the thumb, forefinger, and middle finger of the right hand.

Gagaku music

China and the Asian mainland was as much an influence on Japanese culture 1000 years ago as the Western world is today. The Japanese court took much of its ceremony and music from the mainland, and due to the fact that the Japanese islands were the last places for these cultures to spread, traditions remained strong in Japan for longer than on the mainland.

The court music is called *gagaku*, and is divided into two types:
1 *Komagaku* – from Korea and Manchuria, reaching Japan in the fifth century.
2 *Tōgaku* – from China and India, reaching Japan in the seventh century.

Each composition is really a melody interpreted by several instruments playing heterophonically. The whole ensemble concentrates on the melody, which has to be memorized, not read from notation. The idea is to create a flowing composition.

The pulse remains broadly the same throughout. Gagaku compositions start with a slow passage called the *jo* ('introduction'); this seems to have a certain amount of rhythmic freedom, although the musicians remain aware of the pulse. Next comes the *ha* ('breaking away'), where a more structured pulse develops. Then follows the *kyū* ('hurried') in which many more notes are performed to each pulse, so that the musicians are playing at speed.

These sections are rather like the alap, jhor and jhala of Indian classical music, but gagaku music usually describes scenes, stories or individuals, and there is no improvisation.

Today, court music is performed as dance music (*bugaku*) or as instrumental music (*kangen*). A full kangen ensemble consists of about 16 musicians, playing a variety of percussion, string and reed instruments. To accompany dance, the string instruments are omitted. And to accompany vocal music, a smaller group is used.

Gagaku scales

There are two main modes: *ryō* and *ritsu*.

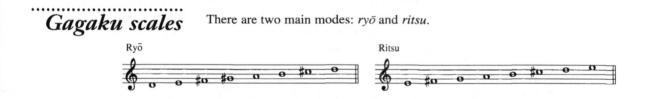

Each has three scales based upon it.
Ryō has:
1 *Ichikotsu*, in which the keynote is D
2 *Sōjō*, in which the keynote is G
3 *Taishiki*, in which the keynote is E

Ritsu has:
1 *Hyōjō*, in which the keynote is E
2 *Oshiki*, in which the keynote is A
3 *Banshiki*, in which the keynote is B

Assignment 94 First play the two modes, and then the scales based on them. Compose a short melody in one of the scales you like best.

Instrumental music

Many of the Japanese traditional instruments have developed from Chinese instruments. It is said that music from foreign courts was introduced to Japan in AD 453, when Korean musicians attended the Emperor's funeral. Japanese musicians were then able to travel to the mainland, and hear the music of other courts.

The *biwa* is a four-string lute played with a plectrum. It is used with the koto in gagaku music. Usually the biwa plays the melody, occasionally adding emphasis with a four-note chord.

The *koto* is a long zither with 13 strings, developed from the Chinese ch'in. It plays the melody, sometimes adding short repeated melodic patterns.

The *shamisen* is a small three-string plucked instrument, very important in the accompaniment of *bunraku* puppet plays, and in *kabuki* theatre.

Wind instruments are always made of bamboo. There is the *ryuteki*, a horizontally-blown flute, and the *komabue*, a shorter Korean flute.

The *hichiriki* is an oboe-like instrument.

The *shō*, a mouth organ with 17 bamboo pipes, is very much like the Chinese sheng. It can play a simple version of the melody or add chords.

In gagaku music, the percussion instruments outline the strong points of each phrase and also add rhythm. Percussion instruments play a very important part in *noh* drama and *kabuki* plays.

Assignment 95
CD TRACK 51

Listen to part of a gagaku piece, *Manzairaku*, and identify as many of the instruments as possible. In addition to three of the wind instruments mentioned above, the ensemble includes a *kakko* (small drum) and *taiko* (large drum). A biwa can also be heard. The music is said to simulate the call of a bird.

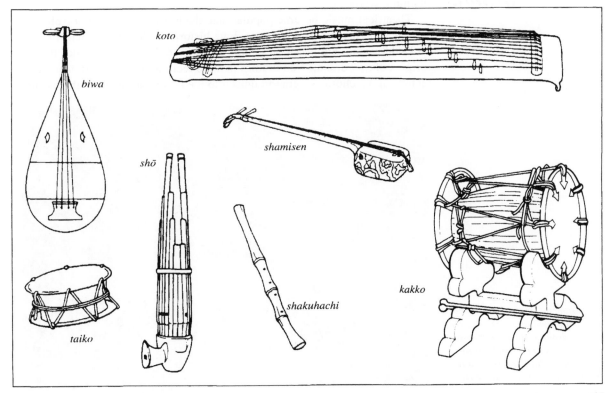

koto

biwa

shamisen

shō

shakuhachi

kakko

taiko

There are also a great many folk instruments. Folk melodies are very popular in their original form, or as songs with piano accompaniment, and also as a basis for instrumental music.

Assignment 96

Here are two Japanese melodies. Form groups and play them heterophonically, using wind and plucked string instruments. A little percussion could also be added.

Cherry Tree – this melody is based on an old court song

Lullaby of Itsuki – this originates from a remote mountain village

Music and drama

Between 1200 and 1500 there were turbulent changes in Japan, and courts were very much dominated by military regimes. This was the time of the Samurai warriors.

Theatrical music became popular, and the biwa was used by travelling priests and chanters to accompany long historical tales. Mime performances at Buddhist and Shinto shrines combined with folk-tales to produce the origins of *noh* drama. Noh dramas involve reciting, singing and dancing, actors, and a chorus singing in unison to the accompaniment of three drums

Instruments accompanying this noh drama are: taiko (barrel drum, resting on its side), ōtsuzumi and kotsuzumi (hourglass drums), and fue (flute); the chorus is on the right

Bunraku puppet theatre

and a flute. It had, and still has, strict rules of melodic structure, rhythmic pattern and design. These factors have had a great effect on the music dramas of other cultures, as well as on the survival of noh drama today.

Popular dance and theatrical music grew in popularity from 1500 to the end of the nineteenth century. Cities had street parades which used large numbers of percussion and flutes. Puppet theatres also became firm favourites, and melodramatic plays developed into what is now called *bunraku*. Each bunraku puppet needs three manipulators. Bunraku became an important source of literature, and was performed by skilled chanters to the accompaniment of the shamisen.

Kabuki drama being performed in Kyōto on the island of Honshū

The *kabuki* theatre also developed during this period, sometimes adapting puppet plays for its own use. Music for the kabuki included the shamisen of the puppet theatre, the flute and drums of the noh dramas, and many other folk instruments, producing a flamboyant music theatre. The music is also sometimes used in concert performances.

The themes of kabuki dramas are often the conflict between rulers and their subjects. The acting is very formalized, and the style has been handed down from one generation to the next. Long monologues are half spoken, half sung, and the style of acting required for the kabuki theatre demands that actors start training from childhood. Study of music is an important part of the training. The music continues throughout the performance, introducing the actors as well as accompanying the dances. Wooden clappers announce the beginning and end of a kabuki play, and are used as a percussion instrument during the performance.

Music in modern Japan

Since 1945, Japan's economic success has ensured that all types of Western instruments have been manufactured, ranging from electronic synthesizers and keyboards to Western orchestral instruments and pianos. However, all types of Japanese traditional music have continued to flourish, and ancient art-forms continue to be popular.

CD track listing

1	*Atsiagbeko*, dance from Ghana
2	Talking drums, Tamale, northern Ghana
3	Music of the Blekete cult, Ghana
4	'Mosese 2000', performed by the group Somo Somo
5	'Duke', performed by the group Kantata
6	*Safari na Muziki* (Walking with music) played on mbira by Hukwe Zawose
7	Xylophone music played by a Lobi musician from northern Ghana
8	'Laminba', song accompanied by kora, performed by Foday Musa Suso of Gambia
9	'Banana Boat Song'
10	'Linstead Market'
11	'Jamaica Farewell'
12	'Long Time Gal'
13	'Coconut Woman'

9–13 played by Elizabeth Sharma (using multi-tracking)

14	Dance music of the *Rwayss* poet-musicians of the Moroccan Berbers
15	Folk-song from Tunisia
16	*Cerga*, Turkish folk-dance, performed by the group Arabesque (Hassan Erraji, Ralph Mizraki, Pierre Marie Narcisse)
17	'Ahbil nra ad dik nmum', performed by Berber musicians
18	Music in maqām *Hussayni*, played on the 'ūd by Hassan Erraji
19	Music in maqām *Nihawand*, played on the qānūn by Hassan Erraji
20	Variations in the same maqām, played on the nāy by Hassan Erraji
21	*Jugalbandi* (duet) improvised on sitar and sāraṅgī by Ustād Rais Khan and Ustād Sultan Khan
22	Raga Bhupali, played on santūr by Pandit Shiv Kumar Sharma
23	Raga Manjh Khamaj, played by Hariprasad Chaurasia (flute)
24–30	Talas played on tablā by Vijay Kangutkar:
	24 Tīn-tāl
	25 Ek-tāl
	26 Kehrva
	27 Jhap-tāl
	28 Rūpak-tāl
	29 Dādrā
	30 Dhamār
31	*Bols* (strokes on tablā) demonstrated by Vijay Kangutkar
32	Performance, on tablā, by Vijay Kangutkar
33	'Hey Jamalo' (bhangra song) performed by Golden Star
34	'Hey Jamalo' (remix version) performed by Bally Sagoo
35	Fisherman's song from Bengal, played by Elizabeth Sharma
36	'Allah Hoo Allah Hoo Allah Hoo' (Praise God) performed by Ustād Nusrat Fateh Ali Khan and party
37	*Tabuh Loma-Loma*, performed by musicians of the temple of Batur, Bali
38	*Tabuh Pisan*, performed by musicians of the temple of Tampaksiring, Bali
39	Javanese gamelan music in slendro scale, performed by musicians from Yogyakarta, Java
40	*Gending Anglirmendung*, traditional Javanese music in pelog scale, performed by musicians from Yogyakarta, Java

41	Balinese piece, *Rearing Horse*, played on electronic keyboard by Elizabeth Sharma
42	*Chinese Martial Arts*, played by the Chinese Classical Orchestra, conducted by Lui Pui-Yuen
43	*Flowing Waters*, played on the ch'in by Li Xiangting
44	*Himalayas*, played by the Guo brothers
45	*Han Palace by Autumn Moonlight*, played by Jing Ying Soloists
46	*Dance Music of Hua T'iao Tzu*, played by the Chinese Classical Orchestra
47	*Without a Song*, played by the Chinese Classical Orchestra
48	*Moonlight over Spring River*, played by Jing Ying Soloists
49	Mitzuhashi Koto: *Shochikubai* (Music of pine, bamboo and plum blossom) performed by the Japanese Koto Orchestra
50	Kazuko Tsukushi: *Nagare* (The stream) performed by the Japanese Koto Orchestra
51	*Manzairaku*, gagaku piece, played by the Kyōto Imperial Court Music Orchestra

Acknowledgements

We are grateful to the following for permission to reproduce photographs:

p.5 Institute of African Studies (Kwasi Andoh); p.17 *above* Britstock-IFA
(W. Rudolph); p.17 *below* Andrew Grimes; p.19 Malcolm Neal;
p.23 Redferns (Carey Brandon); p.34 Deben Bhattacharya Limited;
p.37 Bipinchandra J. Mistry; p.39 Images of India/DPA; p.41 Bipinchandra
J. Mistry; p.45 The Hulton Getty Picture Collection; p.46 Rex Features
(Peter Brooker); p.47 Sonoton (Paul Mulcahy); p.53 The Hutchison Library
(J. G. Fuller); p.56 Redferns (Odile Noel); p.57 Dr R. Garfias, Irvine,
California; p.62 The Hulton Getty Picture Collection; p.63 Zhou Wenju
(Attrib. to), Chinese, United by Music (female musicians playing before the
Emperor), handscroll, ink and color on silk, Ming dynasty (1368 – 1644),
early 15th century, 41.9 x 184.2 cm, Kate S. Buckingham Fund, 1950. 1370
right side. Photograph © 1966. The Art Institute of Chicago, All Rights
Reserved; p65 Zefa; p68 Japan Information & Cultural Centre; p.69 *above*
William P. Malm; p.69 *below* Robert Harding Picture Library.

Picture Research: Valerie Mulcahy

Illustrations: Fran Sewell